Frances Young is now retired, b   in this book with teaching Theology at the University of Birmingham, where she was on the staff from 1971 to 2005. She was ordained as a Methodist minister in 1984 and, a year later, *Face to Face* – her first account of her journey of faith with Arthur – was published, with a larger edition issued in 1990. Arthur has influenced many other publications, including *Can These Dry Bones Live?* (1982), *Brokenness and Blessing: Towards a Biblical Spirituality* (2007) and *God's Presence: A Contemporary Recapitulation of Early Christianity* (2013). Well known for many academic publications in her field of early Christianity, Professor Young was elected to the Edward Cadbury Chair of Theology and served as Head of Department, Dean of the Faculty and Pro-Vice-Chancellor of the University. In retirement, she writes articles and books, still responds to invitations to lecture, and regularly preaches and leads worship.

ARTHUR'S CALL

*A journey of faith in the face of
severe learning disability*

Frances Young

First published in Great Britain in 2014

Society for Promoting Christian Knowledge
36 Causton Street
London SW1P 4ST
www.spckpublishing.co.uk

British Library Cataloguing-in-Publication Data
A catalogue record for this book is available from the British Library

ISBN 978–0–281–07045–9
eBook ISBN 978–0–281–07046–6

Typeset by Graphicraft Limited, Hong Kong
First printed in Great Britain by Ashford Colour Press
Subsequently digitally printed in Great Britain

eBook by Graphicraft Limited, Hong Kong

Produced on paper from sustainable forests

To Jean Vanier,
who asked for a new Face to Face,
and to whom I owe so much,
with deep gratitude.

Contents

Foreword

'Arthur is seriously brain-damaged and unable to develop normally.' This was what Frances Young was told when Arthur was a few months old. Frances, then a mother with her first child, now a Methodist minister and former Edward Cadbury Professor of Theology in the University of Birmingham, tells her story from this stark beginning up to today. Arthur was born in 1967, severely brain-damaged, unable to learn to do anything for himself and consequently dependent on other people for his every need. For 45 years, that is, until summer 2012, he lived at home, cared for by his parents. He attended a local Day Centre, and respite care allowed them to take their younger sons on holiday, but neither relieved the underlying responsibility for his welfare. Then they decided they could no longer look after him as well as they would wish, so he would have to go into full-time professional care.

Steve Motyer, writing on the grief of Mary and Martha over the death of Lazarus (John 11.1–44) says: 'we realise that somehow the pathway through terrible sorrow is necessary, so that God may finally be glorified by our deliverance. And Jesus weeps with us on that way.'[1] Those words say much about this book. Frances has had to face the trauma and grief of the realization that Arthur was born severely brain-damaged and unable to develop significantly. By telling Arthur's story, she tells the story of her own passage through grief, spiritual development and a greater insight into meaning of severe disability in the Christian faith.

I have known Frances as a fellow Methodist and hill-walker from our undergraduate days; her husband Bob was also a fellow under-graduate. My wife and I have known Arthur since he was about five. In the early years we met only infrequently and saw only a little of the attempts to teach Arthur the simple things of which Frances writes, such as holding a cup or walking. Later on we met more often and became particularly aware of how any activity had to be arranged around Arthur's needs. A day's walking together meant someone had to be back by the time Arthur was brought home from his Day Centre; respite care had to be booked up to a year in advance. A cold or windy day meant that he could not be taken out in his wheelchair even to nearby shops or the local park. We heard a little of the debate over the (eventually abandoned) proposal for surgery to help some of his physical distortions; we saw the heart-searching caused by the decision to put him into full-time care. We saw how his care was shared between Frances and Bob and the strain arising when Bob was unable to take his full share because of his cancer and a later shoulder injury. We saw how Frances brought him into family life by giving him his meals with everyone else. We saw the need for patience when giving him a meal, waiting for him to decide he was ready – particularly demanding when time was short. We have seen how, now that Arthur is in full-time care, he still comes home regularly and Frances takes him with her to her local church and on her preaching appointments.

Frances first wrote about Arthur back in 1985, in the first edition of *Face to Face*. In this book she brings Arthur's story up to date. Part of the story is narrative, about Arthur himself and the many problems his care at home has presented, about Frances' own spiritual development and about some of the people who have guided her; part of that story is her meditations on the meaning of severe disability and its relationship to her Christian faith; part is what we can learn from contact with people like Arthur. All of it is important to anyone having to care for someone with severe disability, possibly over many years. In writing about Arthur and in telling of her own path from the anguish of learning she had a disabled son through to her present faith, she provides all of us who have contact with disabled people something that will help us to continue in our work and to understand a little better how it fits with our own faith. It is not easy reading, but both challenging and rewarding.

Most importantly, the book is a love story; not the 'boy meets girl . . . and they all lived happily ever after' of romantic fiction, but the truer love story of devotion and care given freely over 45 years; of a lifestyle constrained by Arthur's needs; of the difficulty of deciding what is in Arthur's best interest, particularly as he is totally unable to express his views; of trying to work out what is making him unhappy.

In a materialistic society, people will ask, 'What can Arthur contribute to society?' More ruthless societies have asked, 'Why waste resources on such people?' Such thinking can lead to the atrocities that appear only too frequently in the media. Arthur can't do any of the things we regard as contributing – running a scout troop, driving a bus or cooking a meal – but in telling Arthur's story, Frances indirectly asks all of us to consider our attitude to all such people. How far do we face the fact that Arthur and any handicapped person is a *PERSON* needing our understanding and compassion, needing contact with people; that his carers equally need our understanding and support; that his vulnerability and trust teaches us about our own vulnerability and dependence on others. His contribution to society is this book and the ideas it contains! Without him it could not have been written.

Peter J. F. Humble

Preface

My purpose in this book is to give testimony to a journey of faith inspired by caring for a profoundly disabled son for 45 years, while also being theologian, university teacher and Methodist minister. It takes up, yet significantly modifies, the earlier account written when Arthur was 17 and published as *Face to Face* (1985) – indeed, most of the first two chapters is drawn from that earlier version, whose climax was my call to ordination after years of struggle with doubt. This version has a different perspective, focusing on Arthur's vocation and articulating the way in which this life-dominating experience has given me privileged access to the deepest truths of Christianity. Inevitably it draws on a lifetime of reflection.

As in the two versions of *Face to Face* (1985, enlarged in 1990), narrative and theological reflection are interwoven in the retelling of stories which have often been recounted earlier in a variety of different contexts, oral and written. Ideas are necessarily incorporated which have been drafted in previous publications and this book, though intended for a more general readership, has inevitably some overlaps with my recent more academic publication, *God's Presence: A Contemporary Recapitulation of Early Christianity* (Cambridge University Press, 2013), which itself drew from *Face to Face* and other earlier compositions. It is the writing of *God's Presence* to which reference is made in Chapter 6. I acknowledge permission from both Cambridge University Press and Continuum (T&T Clark) to reuse poems and other material in either or both of those works. Permission has also been obtained to reuse other previously published material; in particular I note with gratitude permissions from the *Methodist Recorder*, Darton, Longman and Todd, SPCK and the editors of *The Edge of God*. Chapter by chapter, the following borrowings are made from my own previous work:

Chapter 1: the first two sections are largely reordered paragraphs from the original *Face to Face*.

Chapter 2: though set in a new framework, this chapter is almost entirely drawn from the original *Face to Face*.

Chapter 3: the initial Lourdes narratives were written for my monthly column in the *Methodist Recorder*, 1991; material is extracted from the introduction to *Encounter with Mystery: Reflections on L'Arche and Living with Disability* (London: Darton, Longman and Todd, 1997), and from some of the essays in that volume, which I edited; the poem first appeared in *God's Presence*.

Chapter 4: is an amalgam of new writing and extracts from various public lectures and *Face to Face* (1990), as well as 'The creative purpose of God', my essay in *Encounter with Mystery*, pp. 167–79, and the address given at the L'Arche IGA in 2003. Some of this has already been used in *God's Presence*, including the poem 'Elusive Likeness'.

Chapter 5: includes extracts from 'The Mark of the Nails', in *Resurrection: Essays in Honour of Leslie Houlden*, edited by Stephen Barton and Graham Stanton (London: SPCK, 1994), pp. 139–53; material from *Face to Face* (1990); and earlier treatments of atonement in various public lectures and encyclopedia articles.

Chapter 6: refers to the writing of *God's Presence*, to the creation of its cover image, and includes the poem 'Jesus', which first appeared in that volume.

Chapter 7: includes material drafted for a WCC group on disability; and extracts from 'Songs without Words: Incorporating the Linguistically Marginalised', in *The Edge of God: New Liturgical Texts and Contexts in Conversation*, edited by Stephen Burns, Nicola Slee and Michael N. Jagessar (London: Epworth, 2008). The poem 'Imagine' originally appeared in *Face to Face* (1990), and in this revised form in *God's Presence*.

For the most part biblical quotations are taken from the NRSV.

On many pages my debt to the practical help of so many people will be evident. Those named have given permission for their identification; but an army of teachers and carers who have made it possible for us to enjoy such full lives remain anonymous, yet must be acknowledged with profound gratitude.

Introduction

————◆————

It was a day which marked a significant step in my journey from grief to gratitude, from anxiety to hope, from trauma to trust, from anguish to joy.

My severely disabled son, Arthur, had settled into residential care less than five weeks previously. Encouraged to treat this as extended respite care, we had had a few days' holiday, and I'd not seen him for a week. Unexpectedly I found when I arrived that the music man was there with keyboard and guitars, shakers and tambourines, old songs and new, rhythm and melody. Soon everyone was joining in, and I found myself drawn into a community of smiles and clapping, dancing with Arthur in his wheelchair, and interacting with other residents and staff. Yes, before this I'd found thanksgiving and relief that Arthur seemed contented and everyone so positive and welcoming. Yes, before this anxieties had begun to be allayed, and the anguish of loss ameliorated. But that day I tasted joy as well as hope, and began to accept that maybe Arthur would be better off surrounded by those committed carers than lately he'd been at home with boring old Darby and Joan. That day was a significant step along this new and unfamiliar path.

It's nearly 30 years since I wrote *Face to Face*, an account of my response, as mother and theologian, to the experience of having a profoundly disabled child. In retrospect, we can now see that, then aged 17, Arthur had in certain ways reached a peak. It would not be long before he started losing his meagre physical attainments. It was also a major turning point in my own journey of faith, the point at which I was ordained as a Methodist minister. During the years of his adulthood since then we've together had to travel through many more challenges, as well as receiving major new insights and blessings. In the end, after 45 years, came the moment of separation, a final enforced weaning as residential care became inevitable. It would seem appropriate to update the story, and offer again the kind of theological reflection on this lifetime experience which so many have said they found helpful.

At first I planned to retain the freshness of the original account (1985), and add to it, but increasingly it became clear that the perspectives of the early 1980s would not sit easily alongside new material; nor would the second edition's ad hoc addition of theological reflections (1990) provide a basis for a more mature and integrated overview. So overall this is a fresh version, taking up earlier stages of the journey into the present whole, but also interweaving material from many sources, not only the two versions of *Face to Face* but also lectures and publications produced during the intervening years. It's now possible to describe the fundamental change in my life as a move from struggling with the 'why?' questions to grasping that I've had privileged access to the deepest truths of Christianity. For that I am profoundly grateful. The former dominated the earlier versions, while this moves through that to the latter.

Here, then, we begin with Arthur's life, his development and his capabilities, as adult as well as child, and consider his place within the family, his relationships, and the joys and constraints of our life with him. Then we recap the wilderness years, the doubts and questions, and the crucial moments that generated profound change in my mind and heart. Through the publication of *Face to Face* I found myself in increasingly close contact with Jean Vanier, and so involved in Faith and Light, as well as L'Arche International. Experiences in Lourdes and Moscow are related since they were profoundly significant for my journey, personally and theologically. These narrative chapters provide background for the development of a theology of creation which embraces vulnerability, and a theology of the cross as the place where Christians perceive resolution of all the 'gone-wrongness' in God's creation. Returning to narrative, we explore the paradox that love means letting go. Implicit perhaps is the insight that this, my painful loss, somehow reflects the loving of a God who creates by withdrawing so as to allow other things to be themselves, lets go but never finally abandons, and through the redemptive suffering of Christ turns darkness into light, death into life. The climax, to some extent drawing from earlier chapters, builds up a sense of the purpose of Arthur's life – indeed, a picture of Arthur's vocation, not just to be part of my ministry, but to have his *own* particular vocation and ministry in being who he is.

1

Arthur's life with us

─────◆─────

It was in June 2012, when he'd just had his 45th birthday, that Arthur finally left home and we ceased to be his carers. This chapter tells the human story, not just articulating what it's like to have a child born with severe disabilities, but also giving an account of his development into adulthood, of gains in maturity and insight alongside deepening love, of parental ties and anxieties lasting years, of simple joys as well as grief and loss. But we must start at the beginning.

Babyhood

Arthur, our first, much wanted baby, was born in Cambridge in 1967. I had an easy first pregnancy, walking in the Yorkshire Dales and going through my PhD viva only a few weeks before he was due. 'You're lucky,' said the midwife, 'you're carrying a small baby.' That was the first sign all would not be well, but it went unrecognized at the time. An earlier unconscious premonition was when I decided not to call my baby Richard, the name of my brother who'd died of Hodgkin's disease at the age of 16. I'd always intended to call a son after him, but my mother's aunt had been distressed when my brother was named because her son, Dick, had just been lost in the war. Remembering that family history, instead of thinking, 'third time lucky', I suddenly panicked. That was perhaps just as well – Arthur has long been able to intonate his own name, 'Aa-er', but he'd never have managed Richard.

Five days early the waters broke, but labour didn't establish itself. The discharge showed the baby was distressed, the expected homebirth was risky, and I was sent into hospital. Stimulated with a drip, labour progressed, but this full-term baby turned out to be only premature weight, and he was rushed into an incubator. I wanted to breastfeed,

1

but became a prize cow, milking myself with a machine and providing nourishment for several of those in the premature baby ward. Fed from a bottle at the start, Arthur would never learn to breastfeed satisfactorily. With hindsight his learning disability was already evident, but it would be months before we became aware of his condition.

Arthur's failure to take the breast was the first of many emotional traumas for me, his mother. The nurses showed me how to use a nipple shield, so he sucked from the familiar teat but took milk from the breast. That's how we managed for weeks. But clearly the effort for him was too much. He had to suck extra hard to stimulate the breast and then was too exhausted to feed. Feeding times were long drawn out and terribly frequent, day and night. After weeks and weeks of trying he eventually learned to take the breast, but that only lasted for a short time. He began to come off it screaming, unable to feed as the milk spurted out. In desperation, I abandoned breastfeeding. A couple of weeks later he cut two teeth, ridiculously early. That soothed my emotions – I'd felt so rejected, but now there was at least an explanation.

When Arthur was eight months old our GP sent us to see a specialist at the old Addenbrooke's Hospital. I'd become worried about one or two things which with hindsight seem rather trivial. Without telling me the real problem, the doctor made his referral. I arrived and sat in the waiting room with other mums. One woman had a huge inert child lying across her knee. Arthur sat on my knee and appeared to be playing with a rattle. 'At least he's not like that,' I thought to myself. I went in to be told essentially that he was. His development was abnormally slow. He'd been born brain-damaged, microcephalic (that is, with an abnormally small head), as a result of a placenta which was too small and inefficient, depriving him of nourishment and oxygen during the latter stages in the womb, a full-term baby but premature weight. Nothing more by way of cause was ever traced, in spite of many tests. It's hard to describe the stunned shock and desolation, the bafflement as to what it all meant, the inability to ask the right questions, the awful self-control needed to go through that hospital to the X-ray department without breaking down. The reserve broke as I pushed the pram towards the city centre and met my husband, Bob, in the street.

In the following days I went back to the GP, and also to the clinic doctor. It turned out that both had recognized the problem for some months, but had not said anything. In those days, doctors were advised only to respond to questions. In the postnatal period there's a danger of a mother rejecting the baby, so it was thought better not to tell before bonds were formed. I felt let down. Now I recognize that no parents of children with disabilities have good experiences of being told – it's just too traumatic. Of course people are different. We expected to cope with our baby. We read Dr Spock, who reassuringly insisted that some perfectly normal babies don't sit up till nine months – no doubt with the worriers in mind. Later on I could see that over months of real struggle and worry we'd suppressed anxieties, telling ourselves that babies were much more difficult than we'd realized, refusing to admit our own incompetence and, as new parents without any previous experience, remaining blissfully unaware of the significance of the fact that he didn't smile until 13 weeks. Had he been our second baby, we'd have known there was something wrong almost from the start, as the doctors did but didn't tell us.

The feeding problems never went away. Arthur was a very disturbed baby, and everyone assumes that a disturbed baby is hungry. Also, as he was born undersize, everyone kept on about his weight, assuming he had to make up ground. He'd suck down a whole bottleful without coming up for air, and then suddenly regurgitate the whole lot – I'll never forget the time my great-aunt wanted to feed the baby, wouldn't be dissuaded, and ended up with the whole feed all over her lap! We battled on, unaware at that stage that there was anything wrong with him. I became Dr Spock's 'anxious giantess' struggling to get food and drink into a reluctant Arthur.

There's a legacy of this, 40 and more years later. Between us we set up behaviour patterns which have remained frustrating and difficult to break. He's still liable to refuse to take the first mouthful of anything, sometimes holding out until everyone else has finished and then finally deciding to eat. Yet that first mouthful problem shows he has some capacity to learn from experience: there've certainly been odd occasions over the years when I've inadvertently popped in a mouthful that was too hot. Eating is still one of the first things to go if there's anything troubling him, and drinking has been even more of a problem. The roots of that are clear. I never succeeded in weaning him off the bottle on to a cup, try as I would. At the age of four, he still had most of his liquid in a bottle, and sucked a bottle to settle to sleep every night. Then one day the specialist advised that I must withdraw the bottle. He would never acquire the right facial muscles for speech if he was still sucking. The idea that he would ever speak now seems crazy, but at the time I panicked and withdrew the bottle completely, thinking it was the only way. Arthur has had a problem with drinking ever since.

Feeding and drinking is but one example of the fact that, if you can get off on the wrong foot with a normal child, you can even more so with a child with disabilities, building up behaviour patterns that go on for years. I remember being delighted when Arthur started throwing things on the floor – after all, it's a normal stage of development for a baby to throw toys out of the pram, but ten years and several broken plates later one wasn't so delighted. I remember actually teaching him to take my spectacles off, then spent years trying to undo that mistake!

During the early years with Arthur, after the initial shock, I was in fact relatively adjusted and able to accept the situation. At first it was difficult not knowing what it meant and not being able to find out. No one could really gauge how disabled he was or what his future development would be. Consciously or unconsciously all parents have dreams for their children. We had to accept we could dream no dreams. We began to reflect on how important it is to let children develop their own lives, how damaging parental expectations can be. Of course, parents' expectations may provide an essential stimulus to a child to do his or her best, but equally they may have an adverse effect. We thought we'd learnt from Arthur just to want our children to develop to their greatest potential, but the truth is we couldn't help being just like other parents when it came to our two other sons, born in succeeding years. We naturally had ambitions for them, and delighted in their talents and their successes. But in Arthur's case, having perforce dropped those sorts of dreams, other dreams obtruded themselves.

With Arthur, I thought, I'll never have to face the growing up and growing away which is so difficult in the parent–child relationship. He'd always need me. The possessiveness of a mother's love was able to take free play, and with it the tendency to overprotect, and an inability to accept that anyone else could do for Arthur what I could do. In the initial stages I'm sure this was healthy. It was a positive way of coming to terms with the situation. It gave me a purpose, a future in relation to him. It eased the pain and made me believe I'd accepted him, disability and all. For the early years, it was fine, but it had hidden dangers which bore fruit later. And, despite that accept-ance, moments of distress did surface at surprising moments and in surprising ways. I remember watching a mother driven scatty by her child in a supermarket, and thinking that if she knew what it was like to have a disabled child she wouldn't treat her child that way. A few years later, I ate my words, driven scatty myself by the antics of normal toddlers. It was years before I could get cross with Arthur. I guess a degree of annoyance is a sign of a more healthy relationship.

One of the first things I asked when told of Arthur's condition was whether he would develop fits. The specialist thought not. Some months later we were staying with my parents in Belfast, and we discovered him in a strange sort of coma, not breathing properly, going purple. I can't remember the exact sequence of events after all these years, but we ended up in hospital – both of us, since I was able to stay in with him. What had happened was that he'd gone into *status epilepticus*, a state of continuous, repeated seizures. As a result he was deprived of oxygen – hence the purple. The danger was more brain damage. Happily, once out of it he recovered and was soon out of hospital, but from that date till now he's taken drugs to prevent epileptic fits. For most of his childhood, they were under control except when he was sickening for a fever; then the first sign of infec-tion would be a major fit, and as he came round he would begin to get hot. Later, the pattern changed and it became more difficult to predict or prevent the fits. Interestingly, Arthur always seems to have known that the pills mattered. There have been times when he's been ill and refusing all food and drink, but he's still taken his drugs. Occasionally, in a mischievous mood, he grins with his teeth firmly clenched, eyes twinkling, and it all becomes a game. But in the end, he's always cooperated with taking his drugs, if nothing else.

The early months in Cambridge are a blurred memory of pain, of positive acceptance, of sharing with our childminder, who was a remarkable support. She, like the doctors, had known there was some-thing wrong from the moment she'd met Arthur. But it made no difference to her acceptance of him into her family for the half-days I spent continuing research. But compared with Birmingham, the Cambridge days were days of isolation with the problem peculiar to ourselves. It was when Arthur was 15 months old that we made the move. Immediately upon arriving in Birmingham, the health visitor was on our doorstep, and we were introduced to a local mums and toddlers group for children with learning disabilities. From there we moved on to membership of the Birmingham Society for Mentally Handicapped Children (later Birmingham Mencap, now Midland Mencap). It's impossible to quantify what all that meant to me – just meeting other mums with the same problem; one sweet Irish woman had a daughter with cerebral palsy, almost as big as herself, a huge family, ill-health with asthma – yet she was so cheerful, so full of simple faith in God, in life. I recognized we were not so badly off, treasured the very real joy I had in Arthur by this time, accepted there was still hope. There, too, we had our first positive help; Arthur was given regular physiotherapy, and ways of stimulating him were discussed. Over the preschool years, the society's playgroup was a lifeline.

Childhood

So, as we settled in Birmingham, Arthur was through the worst of the babyhood problems, and things seemed set reasonably fair. We went through the 'I will do anything' syndrome, feeling that any effort to stimulate his development was worth it. We surrounded him with colour, toys, music – anything and everything to drag him out of his private world into our world, and facilitate his response and mobility.

Brain cells do not repair, though work with stroke victims has shown that undamaged cells can learn to compensate. So programmes for disabled children were geared to establishing activities which the child would not progress to unaided. When Arthur was about 18 months, and still our only child, we adopted the Doman-Delacato patterning routine, with the help of a neighbour: a method of moving arms and legs back and forth in the crawling pattern. It was believed that patterning could stimulate development over a very broad front. The full-scale Doman-Delacato programme, developed by the Institute for the Achievement of Human Potential (based in Philadelphia), depended on parents' obsessive drive to do something. Armies of friends or relatives were needed to devote their whole lives to getting the maximum development out of the disabled child, lives programmed to exercises and stimulation, 12 hours a day, which meant no life apart from the all-embracing objective. Probably every parent of a child with disabilities goes through this stage, as we did, but if it goes on indefinitely, it is, I'm sure, profoundly unhealthy.

Tremendous care is needed to ensure that any 'normal' children in the family do not feel neglected. I remember the way Edward, almost exactly two years younger than Arthur, interrupted our great efforts to push Arthur's development forward. As soon as he could crawl Edward would come and butt into every attempt to get Arthur to play or move around. We knew that the development of a destructive jealousy was only too likely, and had to discipline ourselves not to thrust him away, however frustrated we might feel.

But this is to leap ahead. In fact, our efforts meant that Arthur crawled long before he developed the balance to sit unsupported, and although he sometimes enjoyed the motion for motion's sake, haring across a room at a kind of canter, it did not in the end have any other beneficial effect. For example, he was unable to take in the presence of a favourite toy on the other side of the room, and then go and fetch it. Indeed, his ability to manipulate toys was always very limited. When he was still in a cot, he had a musical box on the side, and he was able to catch his fingers in a fairly capacious handle device and pull the string to wind the music up. We always knew when Arthur was awake! But he's never learned to produce sound from any other play devices, and apart from balls and what became the favourite rattle, little else caught on. Still, at age 46, he plays with the one and only favourite left, a plastic 'hammer'. He developed a most remarkable range of hand and wrist movements with it, and the gentle sound seems to help him 'chill out'.

Nor did Arthur ever learn to feed himself. Encouraged by various professionals, we made an effort from time to time to get him to hold a spoon. We obtained specially designed dishes from which it was possible to scoop food easily. But somehow resolutions to teach him to feed himself always seemed to break down – surrounded by many pressures, one took the easy way out and just fed him. But more fundamental was the counter-productive effect of trying to drive him. We stimulated in him a very determined streak by those early efforts to get him mobile – at one time, a physiotherapist came to work with him once a week, but she eventually gave up because he became so resistant to it. Arthur has never wanted to be pushed, and he certainly lets us know it. No amount of effort could ever make him 'normal', and a more relaxed relationship is a far more valuable treasure than achievements as the world measures them. Besides this, long periods when he was off his food and uncooperative were so profoundly discouraging. Instead of grabbing everything and putting it into his mouth like a normal baby, he always had to be wheedled and coaxed, and often would prefer not to know. There was no instinctive interest on which to build. The only thing he's ever put in his own mouth is his thumb. And you couldn't even interest him in picking up sweets and putting them in his mouth, since anything the slightest bit hard – even a Smartie – he'd push out of his mouth with his tongue rather than enjoy. Much later on, when sometimes more interested in food and drink, he would spontaneously pull the feeder's arm towards him, and even hold his cup (with a lid and spout) while drinking. But that's as far as we've ever got.

Still, Arthur did have some capacity to learn. When he was approaching his second birthday, he and I were again staying with my parents in Belfast, this time for a month or two since we were delayed there until I gave birth to our second son, Edward. Arthur's great-grandmother lived there too, and at over 90 she spent hours on the lawn in the garden playing with him. She it was who taught him to clap, and still he's clapping – it's been his principal accomplishment. He also got to know my mother very well, as she cared for him while I was preoccupied with the new baby; subsequently it became clear that he recognized her, even after months of absence and in strange places, like meeting her at Birmingham airport. His capacity to recognize people and familiar places has long been clear, despite his extreme limitations in other ways.

Arthur's world opened up a bit more when the two boys were accepted into a local authority nursery on the grounds that both could benefit from contact with a group of 'normal' children. A year later Arthur's school education began, and there he stayed until he was 18. There were changes of teachers and classrooms, but no bigger changes than that. At school, Arthur was helped with mobility, toileting, feeding and other basic self-help skills, as well as doing educational things similar to those most children do in nursery school or playgroup. Some of the children at the school were capable of simple reading, but for most of them it was education into self-help and socially acceptable behaviour. Many of them made their way to school by public transport under the eye of 'guides', but transport was provided for the very young and those whose condition included physical disabilities – so Arthur was picked up at the gate. One thing that dictated our day for years was ensuring that someone was at home by 3.30 p.m. to meet him when he returned. For some time my mother-in-law (Nanny) lived with us and was always there; after she died, we appreciated the reliability of Mrs Walsh, who came three afternoons a week and kept the household on an even keel. Working mums always have conflicts of duty; with a disabled child they do not ease off with the passing of years.

When Arthur came in from school, he would crawl upstairs as soon as he came home and go straight to Nanny's room to watch the television. There were inevitably some tensions from having three generations in the house, but other compensations outweighed. We simply could not have managed during the years with young children without the presence of Nanny and, for five years, Granddad too. It meant we could slip out on errands, have the occasional evening out together, and rely on someone being in when the children returned from school. The extended family makes problems like Arthur containable, even for a career-minded mum. I began full-time work as a lecturer at the university when Arthur was four and Edward two. Immediately my relationship with the children improved – nothing is more destructive than an unfulfilled mother tied to young children all hours of the day. Not that that was ever quite my situation; there was always a bit of research ticking away. Once I was working full-time we had those nursery arrangements; but even so, the presence of Nanny was invaluable. I have sometimes wondered what Arthur made of her death and the consequent changes.

At a later stage, when coming in from school, Arthur would spend time on his 'roundabout'. This was made out of an old Bendix washing machine – the drum formed the base, on to which was fixed a wooden top to sit on, and the screw, which once spun the drum around, allowed the top to rotate as Arthur pushed himself round with his feet. He could sit in the hall at the centre of the house and swing about, watching all the comings and goings. As he did so he would clap his hands, or gaze at the light coming through the fancy glass windows of the hall between his moving fingers. Watching his fingers is an old, old habit going right back into babyhood. Old behaviour patterns survive even as new ones appear.

Sitting there, Arthur would 'purr' away to himself, or come out with his half-dozen 'words'. We first noticed an attempt to copy a word when he was about seven. He always liked to watch trees, and out in his pushchair one day, he responded to my saying 'trees' with 'eeesh'. After that he acquired 'har' (= car), shoo, you, chair, 'orr' (more), 'hime' (time), 'ere oo are' (here you are), and other even more marginal attempts. The most consistent and long-standing is his own name, 'Aa-er', with the right intonation. This soon became 'ey-oo Aa-er' (= hello Arthur), proclaimed loudly as he entered school, and on many other occasions – after all, it was what everyone said to him, so he said it back. This underwent further developments: we've often called him AT or Arthur T (the T standing for his second name, Thomas), and he adopted 'Aa-er T', 'Aa-T' and even 'Aa-fer'. These attempts at language are no more than imitative – his final school report called him 'echolalic'. Sometimes he'd come out with what we recognized as his attempt at 'bed-time' when out in the car! But from time to time he'd produce the right word in the right context, and we'd wonder. He seemed to understand a firm 'No', and would certainly respond to words and actions which fitted his routine, like 'dinner' or 'upstairs'; but probably that's because of habit. Or do we under-estimate him? It's hard to tell.

As a child Arthur had a marvellous sense of humour and could get into infectious fits of giggles. One favourite game was crouching at the bottom of the stairs watching a ball bounce down every step – it used to be a marvellous way of involving all the family in playing with Arthur, with fielders upstairs, fielders downstairs. Another favourite was to make a paper hat out of newspaper and put it right over his face. He'd pull it off with a smile, or if you managed to crackle the paper before he got it off, great muffled chuckles would arise from within. If he was sitting in a chair and you threw a soft ball on to his knee he would catch it and send it back. Even more fun was slinging a rattle around. Unfortunately, his fun-slinging was not confined to acceptable games. You should've heard his giggles of delight when he got his plate of dinner on the floor, and even louder giggles when told he was a naughty boy. Arthur enjoyed a romp, tickling, being bounced on someone's knee. From early on he loved music. When I took him to church, he was quiet all through the hymns, listening and smiling, and then started loudly vocalizing in the prayers, occasionally picking up the last word of the sentence and copying it. In many ways his enjoyments and responses remained those of a toddler and if you got down to that level you could have great fun. But it took a lot of energy. As a child he always tended to live in a world of his own, from which it was necessary to jog him to get any response at all. Mostly he was content just to sit on his own. Later he'd become much more aware of his environment, hearing a door open and craning round to see what's happening, watching other people's movements. As he got older he also became quieter, but he remained fascinated by trees and other patterns of light and shade – the Venetian blind we once had in the kitchen would hold his attention, and later when he sat in the front seat of our vehicle, he'd turn his head to watch pylons go by. We used to say he was the only person we knew who really loved pylons and overhead wires!

Arthur's childhood, however, was not always rosy. Strains could show up in little things. We tried to adopt a policy of living as normal lives as possible, and as long as we were dealing with two toddlers together it didn't seem too difficult. In a double pushchair Arthur and Edward looked more or less like twins and our constraints were normal enough for a family with small children. The first time we pushed Arthur out in a wheelchair remains a sharp memory – I guess it was a moment of symbolic importance, a stage in the admission of abnormality. For life couldn't remain normal. We simply couldn't insist on taking Arthur everywhere we went. There were circumstances which increasingly restricted him as the horizons of his brother widened. Indeed, symbols were to be as nothing compared with the practical realities of a growing child with disabilities, and even they were as nothing compared with the constrictions brought about by unacceptable behaviour, screaming and crying, resistance to handling or comfort. That was the awful thing – the battle of love.

The early years really weren't so bad. Occasionally, Arthur cried and cried and couldn't be comforted. His inability to communicate meant that even though he was for the most part content, that dreadful helplessness parents often feel with a wailing baby was liable to go on recurring. The more we tried to find out what was wrong and do something about it, the worse he tended to get. It was this, writ large, which began to dog our lives. I can almost date the day it started. I was pregnant with our third child, William. Arthur would soon be seven. I pushed him up to the local shops, as I'd done so often before. Suddenly, parked outside the bread shop, he began to scream and cry. I could do nothing with him. A little later, following Granddad's death, we took Nanny away for a week's holiday at Weston after Easter. It was a very mixed week. Arthur was a struggle, and we simply couldn't track down what was upsetting him.

For the next few years, there'd be periods of acute distress, refusal to cooperate with eating, dressing, changing or anything, inability to sleep, rejection of all handling, comfort or affection. Progress seemed to stand still. We were relieved when things were simply bearable: the bad patches were somewhat intermittent, and mostly we were able to maintain the regular routine. The worst feature was that, when he was distressed, there'd be a gradual build-up of distress in me, until I could no longer contain my feelings. It was his rejection of comfort, rejection of love and care, which hurt; it was distress for his distress which undermined my ability to cope. There seemed no point in his life.

It was impossible to track down the cause. People engaged in one helpful suggestion after another. Was it because of the arrival of the new baby? It couldn't be. It'd started before William's arrival. Arthur could hardly have been aware of him anyway – he was not even aware of the family cat. Was it because of changes of environment? Certainly he was more distressed in unfamiliar surroundings. I remember a disastrous holiday in the Lake District. It would've been a nice cottage, if it hadn't rained all the time, and Arthur hadn't refused to sleep or eat or cooperate with anything, moaning and mizzling away, getting worse and worse for lack of sleep, only happy in the familiar environ-ment of the family car – so we drove around in the rain for four days and then gave up and came home. Strange places could have been something to do with it, but it was not the whole explanation; coming home usually eased it, but it didn't solve it, and there were patches of equal agony at home. The search for explanations, the frustration that he couldn't explain . . . the strain would build up – while at the same time we coped with the early years of another new baby, and both of us doing a full-time job. For a while Arthur was on even more drugs – sedatives given to people with mental illness – to reduce the nervous tension; but they didn't solve the problem. The scared look in his eyes would haunt me. As I sat in waiting rooms at hospitals and anywhere else I had to take him, I'd grit my teeth and try to ignore his cries, knowing that to try to comfort him would make things worse, suffering the embarrassment of knowing that everyone around couldn't understand why I was doing nothing about my howling child.

Looking back over the years, and particularly those years of more acute difficulty, I realize that I've discovered how distress can become a kind of prison isolating one from others. When things are wrong, you find people are either embarrassed or they admire you for being brave – indeed, you dare not let yourself down. So there's a mutual conspiracy not to admit your need. What sympathy is expressed you cannot cope with. If you break down (and I have on several memorable occasions), you feel awful. The only way to prevent that happening is to withdraw, to suppress your real feelings, to hide your vulnerable self and put on a public face of triumph over difficulty. So isolation deepens. It's very difficult to ask for help, or even accept help generously offered. Either requires an admission that you're not self-reliant and omni-competent, and it's too humiliating. You respond with conventional polite clichés and keep well-meaning people at arm's length. My experience makes me acutely aware of how hard it is to be on the receiving end. We all imagine that helping people is the demanding thing; but it's far more demanding to receive help with genuine grace and gratitude.

It was during this rough period that we brought ourselves to accept periods of respite arranged by our social worker – just to get a break, a chance to go away and do something different without the strain of Arthur. Every time the wrench was dreadful. I hated parting from him. I still couldn't believe that anyone else could look after him. If I couldn't understand, it was even less likely a stranger could. I was guilty at leaving him in one strange place after another with strange people to care for him. I had to steel myself, grit my teeth and run away. Once away it wasn't so bad. We're outdoors people, mountaineers in our youth. We prefer camping to hotels, and we wanted our grow-ing boys to experience walking, cycling and roughing it, quite apart from our own need to keep fit and ward off decline into old age. At least being away from home and actively engaged in energetic holidays or trips with our other boys, my mind didn't dwell too much on how Arthur was coping, and we all came back to the battle somewhat refreshed. Sometimes I'm sure he was genuinely all right; other times I suspect staff protected us from real knowledge of how he'd been.

Those were the years when hopelessness would easily set in. The future seemed totally daunting – institutionalization for him, either sooner if the strain finally broke us, or later when we were too old to carry on. There seemed no hope of him having a life worth living. I found myself voicing this in an article which received some circula-tion among parents and professionals,[2] articulating my protest at the success of antibiotics which kept children like Arthur alive into adulthood; was there not a moral difference between killing and letting nature take its compassionate course? Next time Arthur had a chest infection, why couldn't I refuse treatment? Society, by its treatment of death as taboo, by the success of modern medicine, was more cruel than nature – few severely disabled people used to live beyond their teens. Wasn't quality of life more important than quantity? When I wrote about quality of life, at least one reader thought I meant quality of *my* life, *our* lives. Heaven forbid! I meant the quality of Arthur's life. How could we justify his continued misery when the future held nothing for him?

Reactions to this article were interesting: some mothers wrote expressing profound gratitude that someone had voiced their feelings; others said, 'Why doesn't she get out and do something?' – as if the deeper questions could be submerged in a flurry of activism. At the time I respected the wisdom of the doctor who assured me that compassionate judgement was often exercised, and it was better not to make a public issue of it. This happened before the widely reported case of Dr Arthur, who was prosecuted by the Life organization for assisting an impaired baby to die in peace. I was very moved to read that Dr Arthur had his Bible in the dock. I didn't think that 'save life at any price' is an essentially Christian perspective, but rather a legalism demanded by those who daren't risk using their own judgement or trusting anyone else to – an officious meddling with the Creator's compassionate arrangements, the panic reaction of those who can't face death because they've no hope in God.

Arthur began to emerge from the dark tunnel, and his hair to turn curly, when his anticonvulsant was changed: Epilim was prescribed and Phenobarbitone withdrawn. Doctors say that Phenobarbitone can be an irritant. It almost certainly aggravated the problem. As usual, however, we're wiser after the event. It was during this period that he lost his front baby teeth. His adult front teeth were enormous, and because his mouth was slightly misshapen, they didn't come through where his baby teeth had been, but cut newly through his front gums. It wasn't easy to recognize at the time, but his behaviour was not unlike an exaggerated case of a teething baby. His resistance to feeding and handling may well have arisen from the fact that he was unable to tell us his mouth was sore and he felt rotten. Because we struggled with him (remember we've had long-term feeding problems), he got scared of what we were doing to him. Unlike a normal child, he got no fun out of loose teeth, and he wasn't distracted from soreness and discomfort by all the other interests and activities that a growing and maturing child usually has. He was as miserable at eight years old as a baby of five months can be, but the effect was more violent and distressing because he was bigger, and had a nervous irritability associated with his condition and with the drugs he was taking.

So our problem did eventually pass, and from a much later perspective I'm profoundly grateful for later years with Arthur. Progress did re-establish itself, desperately slow but over long periods of time, quite discernible. One day Arthur crawled across the room and climbed on to my knee – after all those years of refusing my embraces; another time he tried to push away his youngest brother in order to have my knee to himself. He's always had patches of preferring to be left alone, particularly when unwell, but we learned to take it in our stride and shrug it off. Maybe it would all have been easier if I'd been as relaxed then as I later became. I've sometimes looked back and been overwhelmed with guilt. Of course, some will say parents of children with learning disabilities are usually afflicted with guilt, thinking it's their fault that their child was born as it is. I suspect that many mothers have at some time or other felt a bit like that; certainly I asked myself what I'd done wrong during pregnancy. But I don't think parental reactions can be stereotyped in this way. Basically I was satisfied that it was an accident and not my fault. There was no reason to feel guilty just because my child was born disabled. But I have felt guilty about what I've done to Arthur.

There have been things I've inadvertently done which have affected him badly – even complicated his already difficult situation. It's those things I've felt guilty about. Particularly distressing have been the physical distortions of his body to which I know I've contributed – all unwittingly at the time. When he was a baby I put him on his tummy to sleep. This was then unusual in Britain, but I'd come across it living in the States, and been convinced that it helped with getting up wind and ensuring more settled sleep. But Arthur never learned to lift his head and turn it. He settled in a comfortable position, always facing the same way, and refusing to be lain the other way. He remained at the little baby stage for months longer than usual, and gradually, from spending most of his life in that position, his head became severely distorted in shape. Over subsequent years it grew

15

right again, but back then it was hurtful to look at him, and know one's own responsibility for it. Then there was the way his legs doubled up – the problem was that having learned to crawl at about the age of four, he sat on his heels for ten years. Gradually his tendons contracted because his legs were never straight. It was I who'd encouraged his squatting, realizing it gave him balance and he could sit up and play with toys, or crawl around. But his feet and legs were in a badly distorted position. Not only did all the tendons contract, but his hips were settling a bit out of joint. The consequences would be devastating in early adulthood.

When Arthur was a baby, he used to make himself rigid, like all babies do, and 'stand' on my knee; when he was toddler age he could pull himself up to standing in a baby-walker. Then his legs were beautifully straight. Physically he seemed perfect. Of course, much of the wasting of his legs would've happened anyway. His failure to learn to walk inevitably meant his feet and lower leg muscles didn't develop normally, unlike his thighs which were strengthened by his years of crawling. Yet I know I contributed to his problems; a physiotherapist had even warned me, but I did not then understand the warning. At that stage the all-important thing seemed to be his mobility, the maximum independence we could encourage – and the place where he could develop that was on the floor, squatting on his heels, feet turned out.

In his teens we always held Arthur's elbows and 'walked him' around, but as his legs got more and more bent he became less and less willing to take his weight on them. So medical advisers began to feel that something should be done, partly because he showed signs of acquiring more balance and there was some hope he might begin to get on his feet if it were physically more comfortable, partly because they feared progressive contraction until his legs were so bent he'd become extremely difficult to handle. So after much heart-searching, we agreed to experiment with serial plasters. What this meant was putting his legs in plaster as straight as possible, and then gradually forcing the plasters straighter with wedges behind his knees. It was a long drawn out process, which complicated getting him about, and changed both his and our habits. Arthur has never been one to take discomfort in his stride – he's always tended to overreact physically and emotionally, whether to cold, infection or any other problem. Now he would scream whenever we turned into the drive of the

Orthopaedic Hospital, recognizing what was coming. There was a lengthy hiatus at one point when he developed pressure sores on his heels, and that caused another patch of intense distress before we discovered what the problem was. Nevertheless we survived those ups and downs, and at first it seemed well worth it. Neither leg was ever quite straight, and for a while we were putting splints on his legs overnight to prevent reversion, but he learned to use the double rail on the stairs and walk himself up without assistance. At school he got around with a walker; and with someone to hold his hands he walked down the drive to his school bus every morning, and from place to place in the house.

All those months in plaster were partly my fault. It's that sort of thing that's made me feel guilty: the mistakes I've made, my inadequacy as his parent, my unintentional contributions to his difficulties. Generally, however, life's pressures have prevented guilt taking over. I remember once going to see my doctor when I felt particularly drained and saying, 'I suppose I ought to give up my job. I'm just trying to cope with too much.' He wisely said that I shouldn't; it was very important, having a child like Arthur, to have something else to fill my mind. Besides, my relationship with Arthur gradually became more relaxed, less self-centred and self-concerned. I'm sure this was connected with the fact that I became less possessive, more detached. This didn't mean I loved him the less. What it meant was that the selfish element in my love was purged away. It made me realize how very self-centred love can be. When any of us worry about husband or child – perhaps they've not arrived home on time – we're not so much concerned about them as about our own potential loss. When I shared Arthur's distress it was also my distress, and we mutually fed each other's distress to the benefit of neither. Sympathy can be a destructive and self-centred thing – a kind of proving that we really care. It's only when we can let go, become detached, that we really love the other person for what they are, allowing them to be themselves, and to do their own thing without the binding cords of possessiveness. And that's when the relationship, paradoxically, deepens. The sheer delight I began to have in Arthur was balanced by an ability to shrug off his occasional desire to thrust me away and be left alone; by an ability to get irritated with his occasional refusal to cooperate, and to act out the irritation, diffusing tension; by a genuine appreciation of his absence for a few days once a month instead of the agony it once was to let him go. And I'm sure I became less of an ogre to him – not that he was ever totally negative in his attitude to me – because it was always clear that he responded to me more than to anyone else. But Mum has always been the person who had to do the horrid things like cutting his fingernails, and there've certainly been times when I guess it's been something of a love–hate relationship. His affection for my mother was much less ambiguous.

Three years after Nanny died, my parents moved to live near us. We've certainly appreciated the importance of the extended family. Arthur's long-standing relationship with Granny was cemented further. Whenever she'd visited he'd climb on to the sofa beside her and respond to her play, her singing, her tickling, with smiles, giggles and greater and greater excitement. He even began to demand her exclusive attention, turning her face towards him if she looked away. When he started saying 'Ung-ee' we had a friendly rivalry as to whether he meant 'Mummy' or 'Granny'. I often felt that she had the advantage of being like me, but not having to do all the nasty things to him! Once they moved to Birmingham he saw far more of her; down at their bungalow she and Grandpa would frequently cope with him for a few hours at weekends so that we could get out with our other children.

I've often been asked how the other boys reacted to Arthur. As Edward grew older, for all that incipient jealousy, we began to notice his protectiveness of Arthur when out and about, and when he started school and his life expanded, all trace of competition with Arthur disappeared. In the three years between Nanny's presence and Granny's arrival, he became the 'eldest', expected to take charge when we were out. As for William, he was a special bonus. We intended to have only two children, but in the light of Arthur's condition and the advice we were given to have a predominantly normal family, we decided to have a third. Arthur has been part of his life from the word go. There's never been embarrassment or jealousy. He responded with the utmost naturalness to the situation, and carried this over to an entirely open response to other people who are different. What struggle there was in the family arose from the natural rivalry of normal, self-assertive, growing lads, whose independence we encouraged. Sooner or later they left to make their own way in the world, but Arthur would remain at home with us until well into his middle age.

So Arthur was the focus of care and affection, and the catalyst for discoveries about relationships. Nor was this important just for the family, but for many who came into contact with us and even helped with Arthur's care. A number of students, for example, were significantly affected by undertaking the job of looking after the family when I was engaged in weekend teaching, among them Andrew Teal (see Afterword), and some were involved in taking Arthur away on holiday with the Catholic Handicapped Children's Fellowship. This opportunity for him continued well into Arthur's twenties, since he was small enough to pass for a 13-year-old and still welcomed. This was one of many continuities in his life as he grew past childhood into adulthood, and had to move from familiar environments, first school, then children's respite provision.

Adulthood

So far this has been largely a reproduction of the story told in *Face to Face*, published around the time Arthur left school. The transfer from school to a local Adult Training Centre was a very happy one, and hopes of further progress were high. He settled down and seemed more happy and responsive than ever before. Everything seemed at its peak. After the restrictions of having his legs in plaster, he gradually learned to crawl again, his thigh muscles redeveloped, and he began to sit on the floor more naturally, it seemed, with his legs folded to one side. It took several years to realize that yet again he was establishing a fixed position, which would then mould his body and create further disability – his back was getting twisted.

For a while after leaving school he had no physiotherapy, and we had no more advice from those who'd straightened his legs. Gradually he lost ground physically – his legs became less straight, his joints stiffened up, his ankles became rigid. His ability to take his own weight, to pull himself upstairs, even to crawl, was slowly eroded. He became not only tighter but weaker, and he knew it. He was scared, wanted support, and was worried about his lack of balance. But things improved, a physiotherapist began to attend the Day Centre, some hydrotherapy became available, and we were assured that he still had flexibility in his knees.

Then the scoliosis of the spine began to force itself on our attention, and a rearrangement of services meant we were able to make renewed contact with the clinic we'd been to before. Little could be done except pull sad faces and try to come up with ideas to improve his posture. A beanbag was one idea. We began to discourage him from sitting on the floor in an effort to prevent further deterioration. But we were in even more of a Catch-22 situation than we realized. The nice relaxing beanbag meant he was not using his muscles to support himself, and sitting in chairs meant he was not crawling; so little by little, he got weaker still. Finally, in his mid twenties, his hips permanently dislocated. The process was a difficult one, with renewed distress and resistance to handling. Not knowing what was wrong, we kept walking him around, terrified of losing this accomplishment, but gradually came to the conclusion that this latest upset was caused by terror of taking his own weight, and we reluctantly gave up. A few weeks later, a consultant told us that his hips, now dislocated, were no longer weight-bearing. The mobility we'd worked for, for so many years, was irretrievably lost. He was provided with a specially shaped wheelchair, moulded to fit his body closely, to give support to his back and relieve pressure on his bottom.

So how do you come to terms with deterioration, with yet further loss of hope? Well, you keep trying to carry on with the usual routine, insisting on him continuing to do as much as possible. You begin to adapt, to think out new ways of coping. If he can't sit in the bath any more, how can you make it possible for him to lie in it? Why, you pad it with the impervious bed-mats you usually use for camping. And though saddled with a new stage of loss, we also had gains. Arthur's awareness and response to things were much improved. He really began to look at things, to play ball with cunning and skill, directing it away from the fielders. It became impossible to leave him on his own for hours any more – he wanted company, he wanted to hear conversation and laughter and fun. He liked to go out, and clearly loved the ride around in the minibus everyday to his Day Centre. We could see him listening to music, his face and response changing markedly as the pace and rhythm varied. There was something infectious about his enjoyment and his mischief which continued to delight despite everything. We would smile and say, 'When Arthur smiles, all his friends and relations do too.'

At age 19, Arthur had to leave the children's respite care which had provided him and us with regular support over a number of years. He moved on to adult provision at Kingswood, based in the local NHS hospital for those with learning disabilities. So for the next 25 years or so Arthur's life was largely shaped by the Day Centre and

Kingswood, the latter giving us about nine weeks a year relief, accommodating specific dates when we planned holidays away, but determining the calendar year's rota the previous autumn – life had to be carefully planned ahead. The great thing was that the Day Centre transport would pick Arthur up from home and then take him to Kingswood at the end of the day, and continue to transport him daily to the Day Centre while he was away from home, thus keeping excellent continuity in his life.

It wasn't until well into adulthood that Arthur began to grow facial hair and we were faced with shaving him. At first I managed with an electric shaver, but it wasn't easy and he never looked as good as he did when he came home from Kingswood. Bob got in contact with his carers there, and learned they gave him a wet shave. So Bob took over. We'd get Arthur well-fed and content, then shave him before he left the dinner table. It had to be done with a few rapid strokes in the brief opportunity he allowed before protesting or moving about, and it was just too risky to attempt to shave his upper lip. So Arthur acquired a moustache. I vividly remember some time later, when I caught a glimpse of his likeness to my father, who was likewise moustached, my stomach turned over – my father, a distinguished headmaster with an imposing presence, had died some years earlier, and the combination of likeness and utter difference between the two of them I found hard to take. But it gradually became deeply meaningful at all kinds of levels (see Chapters 5 and 6).

Later Arthur would begin to lose his beautiful hair – unlike most of the men in the family. We think it may have been a side effect of the Epilim, since when he was first put on that drug it had the effect of turning his hair curly. Meanwhile, however, dynamics in the family had changed. Bob decided to take early retirement, I was promoted to Professor and Head of Department, and Edward left home for university. Over the next period, Bob took over as Arthur's principal carer, becoming Treasurer of four different disability charities, and then Chair of Birmingham Mencap. I was largely weaned off Arthur, though when at home I still fed him in the evening and put him to bed. I had 15 years or so of relative freedom to pursue professional interests and commitments, for which I remain profoundly grateful. The rock underlying all the shifting sands of my feelings over the years has been Bob's care and support. Temperamentally he's rocklike anyway, and his experience of having had a brother even more profoundly disabled than Arthur somehow seemed to prepare him. From the very beginning he accepted the situation as just one of those things that happen, and we'd been unlucky. He shared all the heat and burden of the day in terms of caring and handling, feeding and changing, more or less making Arthur his own when I had each new baby to cope with, then taking over as our professional situations changed. He bore with me and bore with Arthur through our emotional upsets. But by now we were through the wood, and it's in large measure due to his steadfastness through all our difficulties, and his wretched sense of humour!

It was in the 1990s that further changes to our domestic arrangements began to occur. Grandpa died and William left home. Within a few years, Granny would move in with us. Meanwhile, we decided it was necessary to find a more suitable way of bathing Arthur – it took the two of us to lift him in. What we found was scarcely suitable for the family bathroom, so it was plumbed into Will's old bedroom, to which Arthur was then transferred. But the bath was a marvellous innovation; Arthur was easily shifted from the old piano-stool on which he sat for dressing and undressing to lie on a shelf at a similar height, and then a button was pressed and the pre-filled bath came up all around him, at a sensible working height: backbreaking leaning over was no longer required from those washing him. A bit later on we installed a lift, which would take Arthur's wheelchair, again a neat device which sat in an upstairs box-room and then descended from the ceiling into our conveniently capacious hallway. Bob had continued carrying Arthur upstairs every night until he was over 60, and Arthur's physiotherapist, who came from the Indian subcontinent, gave the impression he should never give up or he'd lose the muscles to do it – a bit different from all the Western anxiety about protecting backs! In her nineties and increasingly disabled after five hip operations, Granny also made use of Arthur's bath and lift.

Once Arthur's hips were dislocated, a potential new problem emerged – his thigh bones stuck out, and because of the scoliosis he sat on one of them all the time, so that pressure sores became highly likely. The consultant suggested removing the tops of his thigh bones to prevent this, and put him on a waiting list for the operation. As time passed, we found it more and more difficult having this hanging over us, worrying about when it would happen and how to plan for the future. Eventually, our MP, as well as our GP, became involved in putting pressure on for a date to be decided. Full of trepidation we took Arthur to the Orthopaedic Hospital for his admission. The consultant came round with a gang of medical students. As he explained to them what he was proposing to do and why (it was three years since he'd originally suggested it), we began to sense that he was perhaps not sure about it after all. We were anxious about how Arthur would cope with recovery, and whether it would mean he'd lose his capacity to sit unsupported – crucial to the ease of dressing and undressing him. But we'd been unable to explore these questions while the crowd was around. The Ward Sister offered to call the consultant back, and he came on his own without his white coat, and we had a real heart to heart. The upshot was a decision not to operate, but referral to the wheelchair service to review his shaped chair so as to reduce the pressure on that hip. Over all the years since then we've had a few episodes with pressure sores, which always cause a reversion to Arthur's old distress and upset, but with the help of district nurses, the situation has been effectively contained. Thank goodness we never went through with that major intervention!

Apart from this episode, Arthur's life was largely uneventful for some 20 years or so. Feeding became easier, and as one of the Day Centre staff said, 'He loves his puddings!' He would attempt to copy 'All gone', when I showed him his empty plate, and he certainly had adult tastes, enjoying curries and Christmas pudding. We managed to include him in day trips for visits to relatives or family events, such as his brothers' weddings, or Christmas gatherings away from Birmingham. As grandchildren came on to the scene, their visits to us became important. I shall never forget the moment when Ed's daughter, Emma, then about two years old, was told to say 'Goodbye' as they prepared to leave – she went all around everybody giving them a kiss, then approached Arthur, who was on his beanbag and at her level. My heart was in my mouth – he could so easily have thrust her away and pushed her over. But he accepted her kiss, and then his face broke into a beatific smile. Later our three growing grandchildren would have great fun with his lift, and once we resorted to a hoist that became an unconventional climbing frame! I was, and remain, extremely grateful for those settled years of Arthur's adult life. In an earlier age, he would probably never have survived childhood, but antibiotics and anticonvulsants extended his life long enough for proper appreciation of his contribution to the richness of our lives.

During this easier time we even took him away on holiday, something we'd not attempted for years. In 2001 we enjoyed a four-generation stay in a couple of cottages in North Wales, Arthur and Granny sharing a room and being driven around on day trips, while more active people took to their bicycles. A couple of years later, I was joined in Salisbury for Easter commitments by Bob, Granny and Arthur; I shall never forget Arthur's face when we took him into the Cathedral, with the organ quietly playing. He craned up at the high vaults and the stained-glass windows, big-eyed with amazement. Later, in 2005, Ed's family invited us all to accompany them on their church holiday, held in college accommodation not far from Christchurch. In the event Granny died earlier that year, but Arthur came with us. When we had little kids, Bob's definition of a holiday was 'doing with difficulty away what you can more easily do at home'; that inevitably remained the case with Arthur, but between them the family and the community provided help and some freedom for us to get out and about.

Arthur loved having Granny around when she moved in with us – indeed, their relationship was so important to both of them that I knew we should do nothing about Arthur's long-term future as long as she was alive. Mrs Walsh continued coming in to support the household domestically, and the teenage boys next door liked earning a bit by 'Arthur-sitting' for those evenings when we took Granny to CBSO concerts – season tickets had long ensured that we had to arrange for regular evenings out. We managed an occasional day or two away cycling when our oldest friends, Peter and Mary Humble (see Foreword), visited and stayed with Granny and Arthur. With Bob in charge, I could undertake professional engagements away from Birmingham, even overseas. We also managed to travel together a bit, given the support of Kingswood and occasional ad hoc arrangements with neighbours and friends. We're very grateful that we've been able to have full lives ourselves, despite the constraints of Arthur over so many years. On a research contract from 2002 to 2005, I was able to work at home most of the time – just as well, since in 2004 Bob had three months convalescing after a prostate cancer operation. Kingswood came up trumps and offered respite for me every other week. I confess I privately panicked at the thought of being left alone with Arthur and my 93-year-old mother. Happily, everything came through okay in the end.

But, unbeknownst at the time, that was the beginning of a period of considerable change. That year Mrs Walsh became too ill to continue working for us, and that summer Granny developed a nasty infection in one leg, becoming a bit less self-confident. Then the following January she had a stroke, and after three months spent between hospital and a care home, in each case visited by Arthur from time to time, she died between Easter and her ninety-fifth birthday. Once more I've wondered what Arthur made of such a major loss in his life. For over eight years, she'd sat with him at our kitchen table for dinner, watching over him and saying, 'He's still chewing', or 'He's ready, Mummy'. Arriving home from the Day Centre, he'd go into her room first, where she'd be watching the TV – tennis if possible, but snooker was a good second best, and she always swore that Arthur watched the balls. Looking back, I wonder about Arthur's capacity for memory – we know he recognizes things and people present to him, but perhaps he doesn't miss because he doesn't mentally recall? Still Granny always swore he missed me when I was away, and we knew he could become quite emotional about things. One Christmas there were carols on the television. His attention was grabbed by 'Away in a manger'; he dropped his toy hammer and began to concentrate. By the final verse there were tears running down his cheeks. Clearly he was moved, perhaps remembering how Granny and I used to sing it to him when he was a baby.

Arthur remained at home with us for a further seven years, mostly serene, though several winters produced patches of distress with flu or pressure sores. It's amazing how the years have passed, the passage of time becoming apparent only in retrospect. I formally retired in 2005, though remained academically active, and life with Arthur went on much as it had for years. We used to joke about still having a job to get up for – getting Arthur ready to be picked up for the Day Centre by 9 a.m. We had less regular domestic help, but Jennifer, a friend from church, volunteered to help with Arthur, and would occasionally live in with him while we were away overnight. Finally we had to sort out his long-term future without us, but that story belongs to a later chapter. We would never have managed those 45 years of his life with us without the support of many professionals, as well as family and friends. To all of them we offer profound thanks.

2

Through the wilderness years

---·•◦•·---

In the Bible the wilderness is a place of testing and doubt, but also a privileged place where God confronts and calls his people. In this chapter I retell my own version of this paradoxical experience.

From a later perspective it's tempting to look back and see everything in terms of 'before' and 'after'. But it would be misleading to present my journey quite like that. There've been important continuities in my understanding. It wasn't a case simply of dark years of doubt in which life was permanently overcast, and a sudden, lasting clearing of the skies. Besides, it's important to bear in mind that everyday life went on pretty normally for year after year, with the typical tensions and joys, laughter, teasing and irritation of family life, accompanied by the frustrations and successes of a developing career in teaching and research. No one could have lived with me if I'd been in a constant state of anxiety over doubts and questions. Yet they were an underlying, long unresolved agenda which from time to time surfaced and preoccupied my mind, even as I coped with everyday pressures. We'll begin with those doubts and questions, and then recount how I met God in the wilderness.

Doubts and questions

Loving my baby, I thought I'd accepted him. But at a deeper level acceptance was hampered by the fact that I simply couldn't understand what had happened. It wasn't just Arthur. He focused my perception of the much bigger problem. If this world was created by the loving purposes of God, how could this sort of thing happen at all? If God intended people to grow to maturity in faith and love, how about those incapable of doing so?

When we were first in Birmingham, the minister of my church, Chris Hughes Smith, came to visit and some of those questions came out. 'Can't you do it by taking seriously the I–Thou relationship?' he said. He was referring to the great Jewish theologian, Martin Buber, who'd made much of the difference between the way we relate to a thing, an 'It', and the way we relate to a person, a 'Thou'. I felt I'd no difficulty with understanding my relationship with Arthur as an 'I–Thou' relationship, but I found it difficult to cope with all cases in those terms. I now knew about autism, a condition which I then understood as disabling relationships. Rereading Buber some years later, I began to see better what Chris was getting at. For Buber speaks of seeing even a tree as a 'Thou', and making a personal encounter with it; whether or not this is mystical is a nice question, but at least it opens up the possibility of personal relationship even with one who seems at first a non-person. Then, however, I couldn't see it. It was one thing to accept Arthur; it was another to come to terms with the great iceberg of suffering and tragedy he represented. This seemed to resist all attempts at justification. The problem of believing in a good God in the face of the tragedy and evil of the world was posed in a sharper way than before.

Under the surface the wrestling with this issue went on for years, and now and again the questions would become urgent and agonising. They would contribute to the distress. When I was expecting my second child, I didn't consciously worry. We'd been assured that there was no genetic reason for Arthur's condition and the chances of having another disabled child were hardly greater than with any other pregnancy. However, when a well-meaning helper at the Birmingham Society's playgroup said, 'There's no need to worry. God won't let it happen again,' I inwardly cried out, 'If God let it happen once, why shouldn't it happen again? What about people who are carriers of a genetic defect and have one disabled child after another?' I wasn't worried for myself. Indeed, I was surprisingly confident. But I couldn't accept a statement that seemed such a naive running away from reality. The questions were there, and not easily resolvable.

And in spite of that confidence of mine, which was real throughout my second pregnancy, there must have been unacknowledged fear. I'd been very angry about the way we were kept in the dark about Arthur's condition, and as I lay in the labour ward I decided that I must ask the Sister to make sure I was informed of anything wrong with my next baby immediately it was born. It was, I thought, a perfectly rational and reasonable request. I called the Sister. I began to explain, and completely broke down. That second labour was three hours longer than the first, and in the end I didn't have the strength to deliver the baby myself – it was a forceps delivery. It's true that whereas Arthur had an abnormally small head, this well-developed child had an extra large one – all brain, in fact! So there were physical factors. But I suspect there may well have been unsuspected psychological ones too. I was carrying a good deal of suppressed anxiety. The fundamental questions had received no satisfactory answer, and those deeper uncertainties undermined what confidence I had.

Many years later I belonged to a group which met for fellowship and discussion. We began to tell each other our spiritual autobiographies. By then I thought I was finding my way back to a more confident faith, but I began by confessing that every now and again, things happened which revealed that I still hadn't resolved my deepest questioning. A few weeks before, I'd been to Arthur's school for a routine medical check-up. Almost out of the blue I'd found myself reduced to tears. Outwardly, I seemed to be coping with a very full life; inwardly there was still this huge blank. When I'd finished my long confession, one member of the group commented that it sounded like a tragedy, yet what a rich life I'd had. It still felt like a tragedy, a living with meaninglessness.

Sharing with that group was a kind of catalyst. For years I'd struggled with the questions in utter loneliness. It made me confess things I'd never shared with others before. The tragedy was not so much Arthur as my sense of abandonment, my inability to accept the existence and love of God at those deeper levels where it makes a real difference to one's life. I could still make a Christian confession; I still preached from time to time and often found that Wesley's advice, 'Preach faith till you've got it', came true – that it was when I was giving to others, and only then, that I had any real grasp on what faith I had. A close friend spoke of discerning an underlying faithfulness all through those years. But my experience was of an internal blank where God should've been. I had no hope for the future. Despair was lodged deep down inside even if, for the most part, I got on with life, and joked and played with the kids, and lectured in theology, and researched and wrote, passed for a Christian and went to church. Occasionally I'd wrestle with meaningless prayer to a black wall. It did feel like a tragedy. Yet my friend's comment on the richness of my life came across as a healthy rebuke. It was after that evening that I began to climb out of my black hole and find release from the doubts and guilt, fears and self-concern that had imprisoned me.

It's important to recognize the links between doubt and the underlying emotional stress. There's a sense in which each fed the other, and neither could be resolved without the other finding its solution. But it's important to recognize also that the element of doubt was not simply a matter of self-concern. The personal distress was the catalyst for a far deeper challenge than I'd faced before to the truth of Christian claims about the world, about the nature of God and God's relationship with it. Not that I hadn't already faced the intellectual challenges posed by science, philosophy, history, and so on. No one can read for a theology degree and not be faced with that kind of intellectual challenge. Christian faith is not blind faith. It's an attempt at a coherent view of life in all its aspects. If life doesn't measure up to that, then that view must be modified or even rejected, as it simply cannot represent the truth. I'm not suggesting that the truth of Christianity can be proved by rational means. That's evidently not the case. But we do have a responsibility to take seriously the facts and arguments which might falsify belief. Furthermore, the critical process helps us to see what the really essential things are and what are secondary and peripheral matters. It drives us to probe beneath simple 'Sunday school' statements of belief to a deeper awareness of the truths of the Christian faith and their implications. Criticism is often feared as destructive by church people, but it should be embraced and valued for the positive benefits it can bring. Whether we're discussing biblical texts, or credal statements, or the nature of God, or anything else, it's necessary to refine our ideas and test out what we mean. If we have to abandon some over-simple conceptions in the process, so much the better. It doesn't necessarily mean we've abandoned Christian belief. We may even have rediscovered essential insights once central to the faith and later submerged by subsequent developments.

One of the most telling arguments against Christian belief in a loving Creator is the so-called problem of evil. As a student I'd been all through the objections and the standard answers. I decided that the arguments were not, in the end, entirely damaging and that I could go on believing in God. One of the books which had helped me reach this conclusion was John Hick's *Evil and the Love of God*.

This remains a brilliantly clear exposition of one helpful answer. The fundamental case, as I recall it, is that the development of moral beings, the process of soul-making, requires freedom and the right kind of world in which to exercise that freedom. Human beings were created with the potential for good or evil. The idea that Adam, or humanity, was once perfect and then fell into sin from that state of perfection is less convincing than the idea, to be found in early Christian tradition though later submerged, that Adam was somewhat like a child, immature, with potential for development, potential perfection rather than actual perfection. Maturity comes to each person as they struggle against suffering and evil. Penalties for mistakes were bound to be built into the physical order – in fact, pain is a protection, a warning sign. Similarly, moral qualities, like love and courage, depend upon risk and the need for care and sympathy. God's purpose is this ongoing process of soul-making, and this was the best possible world for that process to take place.

But I'd also heard a series of lectures by Donald MacKinnon on the problem of evil, in which he forced us to contemplate the horror of evil and not be satisfied with slick answers. There's a long history in Christian philosophy of suggesting that evil is simply the absence of good; MacKinnon convincingly showed that such a view just couldn't cope with the phenomenon of malignant evil, positive active evil, sadism. I remember asking him once whether he was arguing for an ultimate dualism: that is, the view that there is a power of evil at work in the world permanently warring against the power of God. He intimated that he thought the possibility should be taken very seriously.

Such a possibility does have something of a history in Christian thought, though never an ultimate dualism, an eternal conflict. God in the Judaeo-Christian tradition has always been the originator of all things and the ultimate victor, even if there be a devil upsetting his works for the time being. Lucifer was depicted as a rebellious angel (his name means 'bearer of light'), who fell from heaven. Hell was God's punishment for him and his associates, who, having rebelled against God, now spent all efforts tempting human beings to do wrong and so join them in torment. Such a myth helps to explain evils over which we have no control, but it doesn't resolve the problem of evil altogether. There's still the question, why did God create Lucifer, or let him fall? The Tempter may provide some explanation of human sin, but only by starting an infinite regress – who tempted Lucifer? God remains ultimately responsible.

The Bible insists that God is one, shares power with no one else, and is the Creator. In places, the Bible even suggests that disaster and suffering come from God – as God's judgement. So whatever has gone wrong with the world must be God's responsibility. True, the horror of attributing some of the nastiest evils of this world to God makes the devil idea attractive, and there are some texts in the Bible which seem to suggest that the problems of the world are caused by a cosmic conflict between God and the powers of evil. True, too, the idea of demonic possession is made attractive by the difficulty of apportioning blame for that malignant evil which seems to take possession of individuals and societies, even societies made up of decent, well-meaning people. As Professor MacKinnon hinted, dualism cannot be lightly dismissed. There does seem to be a struggle between good and evil which transcends the human scale. But God is still ultimately responsible, and I've never found the personification of evil as a demon god satisfactory or helpful, nor do I think it's the fundamental biblical view: even where Satan appears, he's often depicted as God's policeman or training officer, the one who sets tests of character, who brings accusations in the heavenly court, rather than being God's hostile opponent (the book of Job, for example). The fundamental biblical view, and the one maintained in the Judaeo-Christian tradition, is that the only real ultimate is God. So whatever subsidiary beings you may posit, the problem is still God's responsibility.

Starting from this position, I found John Hick's book reassuring. I was also prepared to accept the convenient distinction, again an idea with deep roots in Christian thinking, that there's a difference between physical evils and moral evil, that many of the things we think are evil are not really but have a positive purpose. The only real evil is the result of human choice. In this way, God's responsibility is reduced. God is responsible only in so far as he allowed human beings freedom to choose.

Arthur's condition challenged all these convenient assumptions and easy solutions. If God's purpose was soul-making, what about a new human being without the potential to respond and grow, or mature in faith and in virtue? Even if I could allow that there was something good in my relationship with Arthur, that he was a trigger for deeper love, he represented cases where there's no potential, cases where disability doesn't produce greater love but the kind of desperate burden that causes a marriage to crack, distorts the development of other children and leads to family breakdown, or even engenders abuse or disability hate crime. I began to see clearly the profound ambiguity of suffering and its power to discriminate, to bring out the best and bring out the worst in people. I could no longer accept the simple distinction between physical and moral evils because they seemed closely related to one another. The phenomenon of disability can produce a sentimentality which refuses to admit it's an evil, but everything in me protested against it as cruel and unnecessary. And if, as I'd always been led to believe, every individual is important to God, how could God afflict even one creature in this way, let alone the 2 per cent of humanity born with some disability or other, denying them the possibility of fullness of life? In terms of traditional Christian views about God's loving purposes I could make no sense of it.

Catholics have a long tradition of caring for people with disabilities, and I remember hearing a nun say once, 'You can see the soul peeping out through their eyes.' She voiced that Catholic respect for the spiritual element in everyone, the Catholic perception of Christ in even the most afflicted, disadvantaged and outcast from human society. It's a noble tradition, and I now feel there's much to learn from it. But at the time when I heard the remark, it helped me not one whit. It was expressed in terms of the long-standing view that a person is composed of soul and body. I'd learnt through my theological studies that this isn't a biblical view, but had come into Christianity from Platonism. I also knew that such understanding had come into severe difficulties in the modern world. The 'ghost in the machine' notion of a human being simply couldn't work. There was nowhere to locate the soul. The brain is a physical organ with a physical connection to the body through the nervous system. It's impossible to imagine a disembodied person because our physical selves are part of our total personality. Each of us is a psychosomatic whole – that long word simply expresses the integral unity of our selves as physical, emotional, psychological, intellectual selves. We cannot be 'divided' into soul and body. I was even more convinced of this by the experience of Arthur. A damaged brain means that the whole personality is damaged and lacks potential for development. Of course it depends to some extent on which part of the brain is damaged. Some with cerebral palsy have a very high IQ trapped in the body over which

they have so little control they cannot speak or do anything for themselves. In those cases, there clearly is some ground for speaking of
the 'soul' or 'mind' peeping out through their eyes. But brain-damaged
children may have normally functioning bodies (Arthur had the
potential physical capability for walking but never learned to do so),
and yet their learning disability makes them incapable of making
sense of the world, responding to it or communicating with it. There'll
be no eye-contact, no response. In what sense do such people have
a soul? Damaged persons like Arthur often appear to exist in a world
of their own, to be quite vacant and unresponsive, eyes dull and
uncomprehending, unable to interpret the sense-impressions they
get from seeing or hearing. For years Arthur didn't turn to look when
he heard a noise behind him, not because there was anything wrong
with his physical capacity to hear, but because he'd not developed
the understanding to react. It's quite unrealistic to speak of a 'soul'
peeping out through the eyes.

The biblical view of a human person is not consistent with that
kind of understanding anyway. Genesis describes God making a clay
figure and breathing life into it. That's a story expressing the dependence of a living human being on the Spirit of God. Death is the
absence of God, and in the Hebrew Bible what remained of a person
after death was simply a shade of the former self in the grave or the
underworld, apart from God's life. When ideas about life after death
began to develop, what prophets foresaw was the re-creation of a human
being by a resurrecting of the body from the grave and a re-inbreathing
of God's life, a restoration of the whole creature, a psychosomatic
whole. It was later Christianity, under the influence of Platonism,
that reinterpreted this in terms of the immortality of the soul.

Now if all this is right, then the easy option of thinking that the
soul survives whatever the state of body or brain, and that all the wrongs
of this world will be put right in the next, simply will not do. We
must, of course, recognize that physically impaired people are persons
in their own right with the capacity to make their own decisions,
organize their own lives, and so on, and many of those with learning
disabilities have more potential than used to be thought. The development of the full potential of even the most limited is clearly important. But there are people, like Arthur and more limited than Arthur,
of whom it's very difficult to speak of some kind of 'person', distinct
from the brain-damaged body, which might or might not survive

death. The development of personality or mind or 'soul' is just so hampered. To justify their condition in terms of a soul peeping out through the eyes, which will be refined by the afflictions of this world, is entirely implausible. Arthur's distress and suffering made me angry because it could have no conceivable purpose. I once heard a graduate student attempting in a seminar to rescue the idea of soul from the battering it's received from modern philosophy, and in the ensuing discussion I found myself stressing, with a good deal of emotion, the case of brain-damaged persons as an objection. There's no ideal Arthur somehow trapped in this damaged physical casing. He's a psycho-somatic whole. Granted all the difficulties in asserting the doctrine of bodily resurrection, it does at least preserve that profound integration of our selves which is inescapably part of being what we are in this world and in our experience. It also implies the reality of death, and the dependence of all life upon God. There's no good reason for dream-ing about automatic post-mortem survival, either on philosophical grounds or on the basis of the Bible. Life is always God's gift.

And this brings us on to another problem – healing. What sense would it make to hope for healing in cases like this? Suppose some faith-healer laid hands on Arthur tomorrow and all his damaged brain cells were miraculously healed, what then? Brains gradually develop over the years through learning. There are years of learning processes which Arthur's missed out on. In what sense could we expect normality, even if the physical problems were sorted out? The development of our selves as persons is bound up with this learning process. Of course it's all very complex; there must be inbuilt gen-etic characteristics which affect this learning process, as well as the development of personality – my other two sons have been different from one another from the beginning. But what I'm getting at is the fact that personality is not something distinct from the whole pro-cess of learning and maturing. Arthur has personality at his own limited level. He has a mind of his own which can make his carers' lives a bit difficult. But I always found it impossible to envisage what it would mean for him to be healed, because what personality there is is so much part of him *as he is*, with all his limitations. Healed he would be a different person.

Some time back then I was contacted by a woman who had a daughter with Down's syndrome. She'd had a vision of the Virgin Mary, who appeared and told her the precise date on which her daughter would be healed. The date came and went. She concluded she hadn't had enough faith, or had failed in some task the Lord had given her. The whole saga was repeated time and again. Some years after we'd lost contact, I suddenly received yet another letter announcing the date of the miracle soon to be accomplished. At the time I was worried about the woman's state of psychological health. It seemed to me that this was another manifestation of the 'I will do anything' syndrome, and signified that she'd never really accepted her daughter. She maintained that she accepted her daughter but didn't accept her condition. In other words, she imagined that her daughter's condition was some kind of sickness, which could simply be removed. But Down's syndrome is caused by a mutation in the genetic inheritance of the person. Every cell in the body is affected. The whole person is as she is because of her basic make-up; without her condition she'd be a different person. What sense does it make to speak of healing?

My dealings with this woman were disturbing. I did my best to help her pastorally, standing alongside her, sharing my own problem, and trying to help her to accept her daughter in a positive way. But one thing that disturbed me was her understanding of faith. It seemed to me that she'd turned faith into a kind of 'work' and was trying to screw herself up to enough of it to make a miracle happen. I didn't think that was what the Bible meant by faith. Paul was trying to get people to see that it wasn't their own efforts which brought about salvation but the sheer grace and love of God. Faith is accepting what God has done, and trusting God for all that is to come. Faith is not desperately trying to believe six impossible things before breakfast. Yet my own state of doubt and uncertainty made it difficult to affirm the trust and hope involved in that kind of faith. Part of me was as desperate as she was for a miracle, and our contacts made me aware of my own desperate desire to be let off the hook. I thought I'd accepted Arthur; but I hadn't myself accepted the situation fully. I couldn't make sense of it. Nor could I pray for a miracle with my mind convinced of its possibility. There was that desperate cry of the heart, but no faith that such a prayer could be answered. I didn't think her understanding of faith was right, or indeed biblical; but I had little confidence in my own faith either.

Some years later, when I'd found a more confident faith, I preached on perseverance to a congregation belonging to one of the African independent churches. I spoke of Arthur. But again I found myself disturbed when they pressed the question afterwards – had I prayed for healing? I said 'yes'; but in my heart of hearts I knew that I'd never prayed with conviction. Not that I'd now dismiss cases of apparently miraculous cures for a considerable range of conditions. Our bodies are clearly not quite the machines presupposed by scientific medicine. We're psychosomatic wholes, and psychological factors like morale, and faith, clearly contribute to our total health. The healing ministry of the Church has an important place alongside orthodox medicine, and unexpected, apparently mysterious healings can and do take place. But it's still difficult for me to extend that to cases of learning disability. Most of the cells in our bodies have recuperative properties, and healing is a stimulation of those healing properties into action. But brain cells have no such recuperative properties. Stroke victims lose brain cells for ever; they may learn to compensate by stimulating other cells to take over the function of the lost cells, but the damaged part of the brain is never restored. For this reason, as well as for the reasons concerned with learning and maturing given earlier, I simply find cures for learning disability, miraculous or otherwise, incredible. I have no doubt it's possible to maximize potential, to stimulate other cells to take over lost functions, and so on. But cure I cannot comprehend, let alone hope for. These were the reasons why I'd never been able to pray for Arthur's healing with any conviction. To arouse hopes of miraculous healing seemed to me to be dangerous and cruel, delaying the effective acceptance of the situation in a positive way.

Yet there was this nagging feeling – suppose I just lacked faith? Could I actually limit the possibilities if God was really God? I eventually shared this question with the group to which I've already referred. I explained that, when challenged on whether I'd prayed for Arthur's healing, I'd said 'yes', because it was true there'd been times when I'd cried out for it in desperation, with every cell of my being; but I knew deep down I'd never prayed with any conviction. I outlined my sense that God had not created a fairyland in which impossible things could happen by waving the magic wand of faith. As Creator, God is responsible for the way the world is. Extraordinary things happen maybe, but the definition of a miracle as a breaking of the laws of nature is surely theologically suspect. God must work with the processes built into the created order by God's own self, not against them. It's not a question of whether God can do miracles, but whether God does. If God does, a capricious element is introduced, which is consistent with neither God's faithfulness nor our experience. God has set us in a world where accidents happen, and we have to bear the consequences, whether they're the result of blameworthy carelessness or just one of those things. How could I pray with conviction for Arthur to be healed? It didn't fit with my understanding of God or the world. And yet, was it just a failure of faith? A member of the group put the whole thing into perspective by saying quite simply, 'Does anyone expect a severed limb to be restored by faith healing?' Brain damage is injury of that kind; it's genuine loss, real death or absence of vital brain cells. Whatever we may believe about our ultimate destiny, we all accept certain limitations as part of the structure of this life – and one of those is the irreversibility of death. We don't expect even the greatest saint to rise again to this life, whatever we make of the resurrection of Jesus. The healing of a damaged brain is simply implausible.

This long struggle with doubt and questions demonstrates how ambiguous a religious view of life can be. If you take a purely naturalistic view of the world, as my scientist husband does, it's so much easier. Accidents happen and you just have to make the best of it. Acceptance of the situation, courage in coping with it, getting the maximum human value out of it is all that matters. From the time I met Bob I'd been jogged out of the complacency that afflicts Christian groups discussing what difference Christianity makes to people's lives. It's not true that Christians are better people – my husband is one of the best people I know. Nor is it true that faith gives you the edge in coping with the problems of life. It may delude you into never facing reality, into false hopes, into a sentimental and unrealistic optimism about things. Or it may compound your problems by setting up a sharp dichotomy between an accepted idea of what the world is like and the awful reality you actually have to face. My experience proved that religion is no escapism. It led me into ever deeper agonies over the state of the world. It raised questions and difficulties which the non-believer never has to face. For many years I felt it'd be so much easier just to give up on this Christian nonsense, the absurdity of claiming that this rotten world was created by a good, loving God, the illusion that with enough faith in God everything will somehow be put right. But somehow

I couldn't live with that way out. Something in me resisted it as an easy option; there was an imperative in me to find again the world of meaning which had once energized my life, to find that there wasn't just a blank wall or a black hole, but God. I lived with a dreadful sense of loss. My doubts sapped my energy, deepened my distress, my sense of tragedy, my hopelessness. I was depressed by the experience of living in a Godless world. Yet I couldn't just drift into a fantasy world and pretend that everything was all right after all. The challenges were inescapable. I had to go on wrestling, fighting in the dark.

Someone once compared my experience to the biblical story of Jacob wrestling with a man at the Jabbok ford (Gen. 32.24–32). Jacob wouldn't let the man go, despite his wounding, his thigh put out of joint. He wouldn't let go till he'd got a blessing out of him. The ensuing dialogue shows that it was God with whom he'd wrestled, and God who'd touched him and left him with a limp, and with a new name, Israel. I'd never quite dared to see my experience in those terms, but looking back it seems perceptive. I couldn't let the matter rest. I had to go on wrestling. I would always be marked by the struggle. But it's through the struggle that, like Jacob, I've seen God and found my vocation. I too demanded a blessing before I'd let go, and I've received it.

Meeting with God

The place where he wrestled with God, Jacob called Peniel, which means 'face of God'. According to the story, he said, 'I've seen God face to face.' I couldn't quite imagine what it'd be like to see God face to face, and in any case the Bible elsewhere states that no one can see God and live; but I did understand how one can speak of coming face to face with reality, and in that sense meeting with God is an appropriate description of what happened to me.

The problem of God's reality was not posed first for me by the crisis of Arthur. I'd become aware through studying philosophy of religion that there were no satisfactory arguments for God's existence: the whole thing just works out about 50–50, and people make up their minds on quite other grounds. I'd been profoundly challenged by meeting and marrying someone who didn't share the beliefs with which I'd grown up and by which I'd come to live. Strangely enough, it was that experience which gave me an unconventional argument for God's existence. The extraordinary happiness of marriage had so filled me with gratitude and the sense that something had happened to me which I in no way deserved, that I felt there had to be someone to say 'thank you' to. I still think that was a profound discovery, and I'm sure that the core of Christian devotion is wonder at the grace of God and thanksgiving for our creation, preservation, and all the blessings of this life. However, I recognize that that is no theoretical answer to the problem of God's reality. It was demonstrably possible for people to live very good and effective lives without worrying about God at all. So the possibility that religion was all illusion had to be taken seriously. I doubt if many religious people actually sense the presence of God all the time.

The immediate shock of Arthur's condition was a bit like a bereavement. I've noticed several times that God seems more real in the face of death, particularly the death of close relatives. Similarly, my distress had within it a strangely transcendent assurance which lasted for some time. I somehow knew that I was borne up not only by the love and support of my husband, but also by the love of God. I remember talking to the minister in Cambridge and expressing my feeling that I should do more preaching after we moved to Birmingham. Soon after we moved, however, there occurred that conversation (described earlier) with Chris, my new minister. The doubts were beginning to be expressed. His reference to Buber's 'I–Thou' relationship must have meant something to me or I wouldn't have remembered it so vividly – we were walking through the local park together, pushing Arthur in the pram. His suggestion did help with my own problem, I guess; but the bigger difficulty of those who were incapable of any kind of relationship still troubled my mind.

Some years later I asked Chris if, in the service on the relevant Sunday, he could take account of Mental Handicap week (as it was then known). He turned the tables on me and asked me to preach. I could hardly refuse. Yet what did I have to say? My questions were still unresolved. How could I preach on that subject of all subjects? In fact, Chris did me a good turn, though I had some desperate days wondering what on earth to do. It was under that pressure that I had the beginnings of a solution given to me.

I found myself struggling with the story of the man blind from birth, told in John's Gospel, chapter 9:

> His disciples asked him, 'Rabbi, who sinned, this man or his parents,
> that he was born blind?' Jesus answered, 'It was not that this man
> sinned, or his parents . . .'   (verses 2–3, RSV)

Commentators point out that this is criticism of the Old Testament
idea that sin brought judgement and suffering, therefore suffering
must imply sin. What they don't always realize is that the criticism
is still needed. I was horrified once when a helper with Birmingham
Mencap reported that she'd been travelling on a hired minibus,
picking up children around the city, and the driver had said to her,
'What on earth have the parents done to have children like these?'
There must be something instinctive about that idea. It's said that
the parents of disabled children often feel guilty, and I'd myself
momentarily faced the possibility that Arthur was God's punishment
for something I'd done – and rapidly dismissed the idea. That kind
of God I certainly couldn't believe in.

Here, then, Jesus dismissed that kind of explanation, but what
other explanation was offered?

> It was not that this man sinned, or his parents, but that the works of
> God might be made manifest in him.   (John 9.3, RSV)

'What an appalling statement!' I thought. Could it really be suggested that that man and his family had to put up with all those years
of disability just so Jesus could wave a magic wand and heal him to
demonstrate his power? I found myself protesting with all the protest
generated by Arthur. That simply didn't fit with the picture of Jesus'
compassion found in the other Gospels, or with any acceptable idea
of God. And then it began to dawn on me. Not for nothing had
I studied John's Gospel and read it in Greek with students. It's well
known that this story is placed in the Gospel as a 'sign', illuminating
the saying 'I am the light of the world'. As Jesus gives light to the
blind man, so he brings light to the world. But the prologue to the
Gospel (John 1.1–14) has already hinted that when the light shone
in the darkness, the darkness couldn't grasp it, and here we find the
next sentences, pointing ominously forward to the cross:

> We must work the works of him who sent me, while it is day; night
> comes, when no one can work.   (John 9.4, RSV)

Jesus, the light of the world, is to be snuffed out, because the darkness
couldn't grasp the light. Yet everything in this Gospel points to the

cross as the hour of glory. For in the end, Jesus didn't waft away the darkness of the world, all its sin and suffering and hurt and evil, with a magic wand. He entered right into it, took it upon himself, bore it, and in the process turned it into glory, transformed it. It's that transformation which the healing of the blind man foreshadows.

Seeing this story, and indeed the whole drama of John's Gospel, in these terms, gave me the clue, and the sermon. There couldn't be any philosophical answer to the problem of evil; not one is fully satisfactory. The only answer, the only thing that makes it possible to believe in God at all, is the cross. In fact I now acknowledge that some of the traditional answers to the problem have a certain wisdom and do provide partial aids to understanding. But I would still maintain that a properly Christian response to the problem of evil has to begin with the cross, with an understanding of atonement. We don't begin by explaining evil away, justifying God, excusing God for the mess made of creation. We begin by contemplating the story which tells of God taking responsibility by entering the 'gone-wrong' world, taking it upon the divine self, in all its horror, cruelty and pain. This insight into the meaning of the cross (see Chapter 5), now focused by Arthur, would feed into long-term research interests. Indeed, for me work was good therapy. My way back from doubt would be through preaching, lecturing, studying and writing, grappling with the Bible and Christian doctrine. In later years I would affirm that I'd moved from those wilderness years of struggling with theodicy (the question how to justify God in the face of suffering and evil) to having privileged access through Arthur to the deepest truths of Christianity.

Meanwhile, particular incidents marked further progress. I once started a sermon with the words, 'I met God in the Raddlebarn Road.' Yes, putting it like that was meant to startle people. I actually met an old priest who'd obviously had a stroke, limping along with a floppy arm on the same side. And okay, maybe it was reflective hindsight that made me put it like that. But given the circumstances, it really lifted my spirits at the time. Let me explain. For some years, though struggling to hang on to faith in God, I'd gone on taking my children to church each Sunday, and Arthur had simply continued going to the crèche, since there was no way he could learn anything in Sunday school. I'd just had a visit from Chris' successor as minister who tried gently to say that now he was so big, and could be noisy, people thought he shouldn't be there disturbing the babies and toddlers. With my head, I fully understood – indeed, I ought to have seen it myself. But in those days distress was never far below the surface, and although I knew it was unreasonable, I felt rejected by the church because Arthur was rejected. Of course there were assurances that some solution would be found, that Arthur did belong; but the incident deepened the black hole, the sense of abandonment. A few days later I was pushing Arthur up to the local shops in his buggy, my heart very heavy. We were passing the Catholic church when that old priest hobbled up to us, stopped, spoke to Arthur and then to me. He passed the time of day, and then said, 'How lovely to see him out and about!' It was a simple act of unconditional acceptance. After he'd disappeared, it gradually dawned on me that he'd embodied the acceptance of the Church, indeed, God's acceptance of Arthur, and of me with him. The weight moved, and eventually a way forward was found for Arthur to be incorporated into the church family. That's how I met God in the Raddlebarn Road.

Yet I still largely lived an experience of God's absence, and although apparently having some ground of faith it was still shaky when the bad times hit us, and distress and despair got the upper hand. Besides, it was an entirely cross-centred faith. There was little joy or hope in it: the cross confirmed the grim reality of this world. It meant I could entertain the possibility that God was within that grim reality, alongside us, and so hang on to some measure of belief. It was by acceptance of the situation, I thought, by bearing it positively, that it could be overcome. But it wasn't easy. And God didn't often seem very real. Certainly I expected no solution, no miracle; and those years we had to cope with the problems of Arthur's distress, I hardly had the confident resilient faith to do so triumphantly.

I can't now put a precise date upon the formation of the group I previously introduced as having had a considerable effect upon my emergence from those overcast years. An ad hoc ecumenical collection of colleagues from the university, the Queen's Theological College and the Selly Oak Colleges quickly evolved into a theological forum – not of a formal academic kind, rather a fellowship in which our deepest theological concerns and questions about life were shared. It took a couple of years or more, meeting relatively infrequently, for each of us to give our own theological autobiography and to reveal the points at which we had been confronted with our own experience of alienation or questioning or discovery. I was certainly not the only one for whom this process was of profound importance. We all faced things in ourselves which we'd been unable to face, or unable to put into perspective, or unable to divulge to others for a variety of reasons. We didn't at first pray together, though later, as the membership changed, people moving away and others arriving, we did meet for prayer and meditation from which discussion arose. Each of the stages in the shifting life of the group had its own character. Perhaps this ability not to predetermine what the group was, or what it was for, was its most creative feature.

On the occasion when I told all, I don't remember much that was said actually making much difference. But it wasn't long after that I had an experience which can probably be regarded as the fundamental breakthrough. It was only momentary, and I find it very difficult to place in terms of time of day or context in the life of the family. But I know precisely what chair I was sitting in, and that I was sitting on the edge of the chair about to go off and do something or other around the house. It was one of those 'loud thoughts', that seem to have no context: 'It doesn't make any difference to me whether you believe in me or not.' I had a sense of being stunned, of being put in my place. It's difficult to see why really. It's a theological commonplace, after all, and I don't think I'd thought for a very long time that my intellect could solve the problems. It was all so very ordinary, too. Nothing dramatic happened. I got up and got on with whatever I was going to do. I have not, however, seriously doubted the reality of God since that moment. It's become one of those things whose significance has constantly expanded as further reflection has taken place. At that point I didn't discover God. God confronted me. I was brought face to face with God's reality, and had to recognize that the divine reality couldn't depend on my capacity to believe it. If there is a 'before' and 'after', that's the most significant moment; but it's not the whole story.

The other really significant event I can more or less date. It was late November 1979. I'd been to Kingswinford, in the Black Country, to take an extramural class. The class, held on Methodist premises, had as its nucleus the lay preachers of the local circuit, though being a university class it was open to anyone from the general public. During my second series with the class, I was tracing with them the history of how the creeds came to be formed, and discussing the basic issues involved in debates about Christian doctrine. That particular evening we'd had a good meeting, and I suppose I was on a bit of a 'high'. I've always felt strongly about the need for real theological discussion and awareness in the Church. Here it had happened; and included in the group were interested non-Christians.

At a particular set of traffic lights in Dudley, another 'loud thought' hit me: 'You should get ordained.' Between there and my home I had the whole of my life laid before me, and it seemed as if this was what it had all been leading up to. I don't know how I drove home – I must have been on automatic pilot. I was filled with an overwhelming joy and excitement, a sense of profound fulfilment, of the integration of every aspect of my life. It's been tempting to think of it as a Damascus road experience, but I've always said that a bit tongue in cheek. After all, I wasn't blinded or I'd have landed in the ditch and there'd be nothing further to tell. Besides, I've long had a suspicion of dramatic emotional experiences. They could so easily be explained away psychologically. In the next few weeks I managed to suppress what had happened and tell myself it was all because I'd just had my fortieth birthday. On that day I'd said to a friend that, whereas I'd been very depressed on my thirtieth, I now felt exhilarated. I felt I was at last tooled up to do some worthwhile theological writing and had put the problems of the past behind me. So I let it all simmer down. I let all the objections and difficulties have their weight – and there were plenty.

But it didn't go away. By this time our youngest son was five, and on Christmas Day we expected two lively boys to invade our bed with their stockings and the contents thereof. We just hoped it wouldn't be too early! It didn't happen at all. The two of them played together and we were left alone. Suddenly I realized this was the moment to tell Bob what I'd been thinking. To my utter amazement, he raised no objections and simply said, 'It seems the fulfilment of everything you do.' That was an extraordinary Christmas. I was inwardly full of wonder and praise all day. In fact, from that moment in Dudley I'd been filled with an inexplicable joy, a song in my heart, which was to continue for months. It was a dramatic difference from the inner gloom and hopelessness of the past. Whereas I'd been anxious about the future, now I suddenly felt that, if this was right, the future must work out somehow. What had happened was such a surprise, anything could happen.

Not that it came entirely out of the blue. When I'd been a student 20 years previously, I would certainly have offered myself as a candidate for the ministry if it had been possible for a woman to do so. I had in any case gone on to read theology after I'd finished my initial classics degree, having very little idea where it would lead, but convinced it was the right thing to do. Then my life had taken an unexpected course, through my marriage and the consequent decision to try and follow an academic career, like my husband. Throughout all those years I'd always had the question niggling away – what was God's will? Was I doing the right thing? How did one find out what was God's will? Such uncertainties continued to oscillate around through the years of doubt.

Now, I had a vision. The vision came out of the circumstances in which I'd received the call. Somehow my life's work was to do with bridging the gap between the world of academic theology and the Church – I felt convinced that it meant *both* that I seek ordination as a Methodist minister *and* that I stay in my university post. But the relevant thing here is to try and sort out what it had to do with Arthur. One of the questions I was asked as I passed through committees on the way to acceptance as a candidate for ordination concerned my domestic situation and Arthur in particular. I was able to affirm that, even though I couldn't predict what the situation would be when Arthur left school, I was convinced it would work out somehow. My fears about the future had disappeared in a newfound trust, hope and serenity, an openness to new possibilities, a readiness to take risks and let the unexpected happen. I couldn't rule out the possibility that, even though I was sure I should remain in university teaching for the present, I might eventually be led into pastoral ministry. The future was no longer a fearful prospect, but an open vista. I also insisted that Arthur would be part of my ministry. What I consciously meant was that the experience of Arthur had marked me, and changed me, and given me things I wouldn't have otherwise had; but my words were to be fulfilled in concrete ways which I couldn't foresee. The most important thing was that I found myself able to give thanks, even for Arthur, and for the years of doubt and testing, which made the new experience of trust and hope so precious and profound. It was no longer a case of simply accepting Arthur, but of rejoicing in Arthur.

In fact, it was the sense of vocation which changed me. I was overwhelmed by the sense that God had loved me all along, and somehow everything fell into place. It seemed as though there'd been a hidden purpose running through everything. It suddenly struck me that my brother, Richard, after whom I'd nearly named Arthur, had been convinced of a call to the ministry. It seemed extraordinary that I should be fulfilling his vocation, especially since his death had also been the occasion which led my other brother to take over his instrument, the cello, and he'd become the principal cellist of a professional orchestra. Somehow between us we'd fulfilled what the lost member of the family might have been. Yet this was not the outcome of conscious planning or intention. I could no longer shrug off the idea of providence, no matter how difficult it be to give an account of how it might work. Above all, I felt extraordinary exultation. It was sheer amazement that one who'd so little deserved it had been brought through such a wilderness of desolation and loneliness, and had never in fact been left alone but always loved and guided. Of course, one doesn't go on living at that level of intensity for ever, but the peculiar sensitivity of those months when I lived with a song in my heart did leave me changed. The clouds of distress and hopelessness would return; but were more easily dispersed. A new mother rode the trials of those months with Arthur's legs in plaster, sat up all night with him when he was distressed, and took it all with a new and profound calm. Guilt seemed purged away. It was possible to live with uncertainty about the future, because who could guess the extraordinary things that lay in the future anyway? I began to experience a release of inhibitions, an overflow of love towards other people, such as I'd not felt before. The burden on the pilgrim's back had been untied and had rolled off.

The years of preparation and training for ordination began, alongside existing professional and family commitments. My affirmation that Arthur would be part of my ministry came true in unexpected ways. I was required to gain some pastoral experience during the Easter vacation in an inner-city church in Birmingham. One afternoon I called on a member of the congregation, Mrs Pemberton. I was shown to the front room, full of photographs of her family, and we began to swap information about our children. When I mentioned Arthur and explained his condition, she suddenly said, 'I have a child like that too.' It turned out he'd been in a special hospital for some years. He was a big lad with cerebral palsy, impossible for her to handle. She'd never told anyone at church about him. She used to visit him – a friend from her husband's work had taken them over on a Sunday quite regularly. But now her husband was out of work. She couldn't get all the way to Kidderminster. She hadn't seen him since July. Gradually, her pain and her questions – why do these things happen? – came pouring out. My story was a catalyst for her story.

So I arranged to spend Holy Saturday driving her to Kidderminster to see her son. The way was familiar enough – Arthur and I had been many times to see our consultant. As it happened, I'd expected to be on my own that weekend – the family were going to my parents for Easter, while I stayed to fulfil my ministerial obligations. But in the event, Arthur still had both legs in plaster, it was impossible to take him to Belfast by public transport, and I needed the car. Somehow I had to manage Arthur alongside the Easter commitments at the church. So on Holy Saturday, Arthur came in the car to Kidderminster, and we each met the other's son. She brought along a younger boy, about 12, to visit his disabled brother. It was a beautiful day, and on the way back we stopped at the Clent Hills. We left Arthur in the car, and walked up the hill a little way. Her boy rolled over and over on the grass with delight, and when we came down, she bought Arthur an ice cream. On Easter Sunday, Arthur joined the church breakfast after early Communion. Mrs Pemberton sat next to him, and took great delight in him. It was as though his presence liberated her, and she was able to take the lead in integrating him into the church family. At the family service later in the morning, to my delight and surprise, a member of the congregation pushed him up to the communion rail so that he, too, shared the blessing of the children. Arthur really was part of my ministry that weekend, and I received more than I gave. Subsequently I was able to sort out arrangements for Mrs Pemberton to visit her son every other Sunday. Using his mobility allowance the hospital was able to finance a taxi once a fortnight to convey his mother and a friend there and back. It became a shared joy for her and another church member. So through Arthur, we both experienced what the church can be at its best, a community of love and care and support.

I then found the inner strength to learn chaplaincy work by being placed at Monyhull, the local hospital for mentally handicapped adults (to use the terminology then current – now neither the language nor the hospital is in use). I found again that I was receiving more than I gave. To be obliged once a week to switch off from the rush of life

– teaching, family pressures – and just go to be with people for whom life was basic and simple, for some of whom verbal communication was difficult or impossible, became profoundly important. A little old lady, deaf and speechless, played peep-bo with a cuddly scarf, and the two of us were close in our smiles and embraces of affection. Another more capable lady took me into her room and showed me all her things; pointing to a poster of Our Lady she said, 'She's my friend.' Another old lady spent all her time knitting, mostly blankets and clothes for her doll; the doll was her child, spoken of with the affection and annoyance of a mother: 'She's naughty sometimes, you know.' They shared themselves with me, each a character in their own right, in spite of decades of institutionalization. Then there was Denis. Sister suggested I might take one or two who didn't get out much to the hospital social centre. Denis had no speech and seemed to sit all day with a rather glum look on his face, playing with his fingers. When I suggested we might go out, however, he leapt to his feet, clearly understanding language even if he had none. We went to his room and he led me to his wardrobe. We put on his coat and began to walk across the campus, but we never got to the social centre. Every time we went out, he steered away from it. He liked to be out in the air. He liked to stroke the donkeys. And on each occasion at some point on our walk, his set face would break into a heavenly smile.

> Silent, bent, morose he seems to sit
> In a world of his own,
> Yet responds to the tone
> Of invitation.
> Perambulation,
> Holding hands round the grounds,
> No response to the sounds
> Of conversation.
> Silent, bent, morose he seems to be,
> In his world, yet with me.
>
> Smiling, bright, his face appears to lift
> At a thought of his own,
> A mysterious lone
> Appreciation.
> A celebration,

Holding hands round the grounds,
No response to the sounds
Of conversation.
Sharing, close, apart he seems to be,
In his world, yet with me.
Strange beauty
Of simplicity.

Soon I began to go on Sundays to help with the ecumenical Eucharist in the church on the hospital campus. At first I sat in the congregation, usually with one of the residents I'd got to know. I found myself experiencing a very profound identification with these people, knowing that here were some of the most vulnerable persons in our society, yet each was a self, each had value, and before God we were all equally vulnerable human beings in need of God's grace. Even more moving was sharing in the administration of the sacrament. The rush to the rail, the grateful 'thank you', the simple receptivity, seemed to bring a new depth to what we shared together. One of my greatest joys was the participation of my youngest son. William came along on one occasion to help teach a new song. After that he came again and again, because he loved to be worshipping with these people. On the last occasion, as I tried to set up an ad hoc simple drama to get the point of the lesson across, he was a willing assistant, acting as page and steering the volunteers who participated in the right direction. Later in the service I noticed that one person, whose family had a connection with my own family but with whom I'd failed to make any meaningful contact, lent across and asked my son to find his place in the hymn book. I was deeply touched.

Though reshaped here in terms of the paradoxical experience of the wilderness – the place of testing and doubt, but also the place where you discover the reality and love of God – everything in this chapter has been told before in *Face to Face* (1985), which was written in the months around my ordination and published the following year. There's a sense in which my vocation was its climax, the resolution of my anxieties and doubts its principal theme. It seemed to reach a kind of closure. But it would prove to be the starting point of a new pilgrimage, and the gradual realization over years that Arthur's vocation had to move into the centre. This would be a significant consequence of its publication, as the next chapter will show. One aspect of this new journey, however, was anticipated already, to be deepened and reclaimed later. It was my discovery of Mary.

Some 18 months before my ordination in 1984, the local convent invited all the residents of Selly Park to a carol service during the week after Christmas. I took Arthur along in his wheelchair. He loves singing and music. There in the chapel I was very conscious of his presence, especially since many people there didn't know him, and it's impossible to keep him quiet. In the chapel was a statue of Our Lady. As I pushed Arthur back up the road to our house this poem just came to me:

> Mary, my child's lovely.
> Is yours lovely too?
> Little hands, little feet,
> Curly hair, smiles sweet.
>
> Mary, my child's broken.
> Is yours broken too?
> Crushed by affliction,
> Hurt by rejection,
> Disfigured, stricken,
> Silent submission.
>
> Mary, my heart's bursting.
> Is yours bursting too?
> Bursting with labour, travail and pain.
> Bursting with agony, ecstasy, gain.
> Bursting with sympathy, anger, compassion.
> Bursting with praising Love's transfiguration.
>
> Mary, my heart's joyful.
> Is yours joyful too?

Little did I realize how important this ecumenical insight would become.

3

L'Arche, Lourdes, and Faith and Light

The publication of *Face to Face* led to many requests to speak about disability in a variety of contexts, and this would eventually lead to the expanded version, published in 1990. Meanwhile, however, one thing leads to another: one such invitation was to give the Keswick Hall lecture at the University of East Anglia in 1989; a tape of that lecture was given to Jean Vanier, and he initiated correspondence with me.

For those who have not heard of Jean Vanier, he's the founder of L'Arche, where people live in community with persons who have a learning disability. Of French-Canadian origin, he found his vocation in the 1960s through befriending and living with Raphael and Philippe, men from an institution. From them he learned about welcome and respect for people of all kinds. Gradually a worldwide network of residential communities grew up. Faith and Light is a parallel network of non-residential community groups, made up of people with and without learning disabilities, of families and friends. I had long known of Jean, his founding of the L'Arche communities and his book, *Community and Growth*. My first actual meeting with this giant of a man, physically and spiritually, was at Church House, Westminster, where we were both present to celebrate a significant anniversary of L'Arche in the UK. I cherish the memory of a brief but very personal meeting with him, apart from the public gathering at which we had both been invited to speak. Little did I know how much the privilege of his friendship would affect my life.

Lourdes

Easter 1991 was the Faith and Light twentieth-anniversary pilgrimage to Lourdes. *Foi et Lumière* (Faith and Light) had begun in 1971, after a French diocese had arranged a pilgrimage to Lourdes but refused to include a family with two children who had learning disabilities. Hearing of this, Marie-Hélène Matthieu and Jean Vanier determined they would set up a pilgrimage for such families. Material was provided for small groups of people to begin gathering together in preparation. After that first pilgrimage, everyone wanted to continue in their little communities, often gathered around the Mass. By 1991 the movement had spread all over the world, like L'Arche, and also like L'Arche had an ecumenical dimension.

So on Easter Monday 1991, the sun was streaming out of a blue sky on a vast crowd with colourful banners, 20,000 or so, half of them persons with learning disabilities. Over the microphone sounded a voice, in English, then French, then Spanish:

> On the first day of the week Mary Magdalene came to the tomb.

Two women appeared on the stage and mimed the actions, one guiding the other, a woman with a learning disability, dressed in blue to play Mary.

> It was very early in the morning, still dark. The stone had been rolled away from the tomb. The tomb was empty. Mary was very sad. She stood outside the tomb crying, 'They have taken away my Lord and I do not know where they have laid him.'

A man with Down's syndrome appeared wrapped in a cloak.

> She turned round and saw Jesus standing there. She didn't know it was Jesus. She thought it was the gardener. Jesus asked, 'Woman, why are you weeping? Whom do you seek?'

'Mary' fell to her knees.

> Mary said to him, 'Sir, if you have carried him away, tell me where you have laid him, and I will take him away.' And Jesus said, 'Maria.'

'Jesus' raised his arms. The cloak fell from his shoulders to reveal his white robe. He took 'Mary's' hands and lifted her.

> And Mary said, 'Rabboni.' Jesus said, 'Go and tell my brothers.'

He pointed out a group in the corner of the stage. 'Mary' went to fetch them.

> 'I have seen the Lord. Come and see.'

They knelt before 'Jesus'. Then 'Jesus' lifted each up and embraced them in turn, first the woman Methodist minister, then the cardinal, then the Roman Catholic bishop, then the Anglican bishop.

He says to them, 'Love one another as I have loved you.'

They embraced one another, cheek to cheek, and then in Italian, French, English and Spanish the church representatives said, 'Let us pray that we may be one in the love of Jesus.' They blessed the crowd and 20,000 people shared the Peace. This was the climax of a most extraordinary ecumenical Easter. The symbolism of churches brought together by those most excluded in our success-oriented culture couldn't have been more tellingly portrayed. And I was the one who happened to be there to represent evangelical Protestantism.

That Monday I'd woken at 4 a.m., and not being able to sleep I got up and went through the darkness to the Grotto. I needed to deal with an awful lot of questions and reservations that had been un-attended to in the busyness of that period from Maundy Thursday to Easter Sunday. I sat in the cold and looked at that unprepossessing cave, and the damp porous limestone rock from which a natural spring had started to flow in the middle of the last century. I didn't particularly warm to the statue of Mary who'd appeared there to Bernadette, and as for the great tier of candles and the pious genuflec-tions and kisses, they were disturbing. I needed to gather myself and face the mystery of so much arising from a story so easily explained away. After all, there is a perfectly simple geological explanation of the spontaneous appearance of the spring, and as for visions – who can prove them to anyone else? I had come with suspicions of credulity, with the revulsion against 'idolatry' and the resistance to vicarious religious experience characteristic of Protestantism.

But I'd discovered I couldn't run away from the challenge of some-thing that seemed fundamentally good. I needed space for reflection. By the time a priest from Eastern Europe was celebrating Mass in the cave and giving thanks for the end of persecution, I had reached the point of repenting of my Protestant arrogance and giving thanks for the obedience that had been demanded of me that week. For I'd been required to join 100 or so Catholic priests in actions strange to me. I'd been swept into the unknown, into a kind of 'emptiness', unable to receive Communion or sustain prayer in a vast stage-managed series of Holy Week services in an underground basilica, a concrete stadium holding 25,000 people. Yet there were extraordinary moments.

On Good Friday it had been unexpectedly moving to carry a wooden cross in procession as the crowds clapped; then strangely humbling to stand, like 49 other ministers, by one of the 50 pillars and while a recorded Paul Robeson sang, 'Were you there when they crucified my Lord?' to hold on to the cross (and it was quite hard work!) while a queue of people came to touch it, venerate it, kiss it. To have been on the other side, expected to venerate, would have been impossible, but here I was charged with the task of bearing the cross, so as to enable others to do what they had to do to know the reality of their salvation.

It was with some reluctance that the following evening at the Easter vigil I'd gone to join the priests in sprinkling holy water over the crowds. But the service began with the passing of the light of Christ, from the Paschal candle to each candle in the hand of each person in the huge crowd, and as the Alleluias rose and faces became transfigured, I too had been uplifted; the aspersion turned into delight and joy as I dipped the leafy twig in the bowl and scattered the rain of baptismal blessing, remembering how the early Church baptized converts on Easter Eve, so that they died and rose with Christ. For the people sought and welcomed the water, even though it was sprinkled by a strange clerically dressed woman rather than the familiar priest.

These were new experiences of ministry, made possible because Faith and Light were determined to embrace those of us ordained in other churches, even women, as far as possible within the disciplinary rules of the Catholic Church. To have refused would have been turning one's back on the right hand of fellowship, and obedience had been strangely rewarded.

So, back at the Grotto on Easter Monday morning, I still felt cold – there was nothing to warm my heart. I found myself praying the Methodist Covenant prayer, 'Let me be full, let me be empty', and I knew that those days had been a process of self-emptying. I forced myself as a matter of discipline to stay until the end of the Great Prayer of Consecration, but as people began to receive Communion, I slipped away into the darkness. I went to one of the taps that makes the freezing spring water available to the people. I washed my hands and face, receiving purification after my penance. Then hurled myself up the steps – up and up, racing away from the misty, cold, early morning darkness and the huge emptiness, up and up, breathless, trying to get my circulation going.

At the top I found lights on in the Basilica Supérieure. In I went. Suddenly it was warm, and it felt like home. Yesterday I'd preached in this place for Easter Communion (Anglican rite in a Catholic basilica!). The statue of the Virgin shone bright through the halo of misted-up spectacles, and peace began to fill my heart.

Some hours later, in the sunshine, came the joy. With the cardinal and the bishops I blessed the crowd, and descended from the platform to be met by Jean Vanier. In his embrace I breathed a deep heartfelt thanks for inviting me to be there. I'd hesitated some time before accepting. But I wouldn't have missed it for the world. Quite apart from my personal pilgrimage through those days, the power of that symbol would have been enough: it's because of Arthur and 'Jesus with Down's syndrome' that on that occasion representative church leaders embraced one another and shared the Peace. Not for nothing did the crowd sing, 'All over the world the Spirit is moving'.

Jean had invited me to give a *conférence* (talk) on 'Spirituality for Parents'. It was to be on Holy Saturday, one of several sessions in English, running parallel with sessions in French, Spanish, Italian – even Arabic. After much reflection I agreed to go, if I could take a colleague with me. And, as already described, we were affirmed at every turn and had a very busy time. I had not only been anxious at the possibility of feeling excluded in such an intensely Catholic environment; I'd also feared new levels of pain for myself. A place with a reputation for miracles could have felt very threatening, churning up memories and impossible desires and old wounds, even if I could not really envisage physically taking Arthur with me. Besides, it's sometimes at considerable cost that I speak publicly of the dark places of the soul that I've visited. Strangely, I was both prepared for and yet surprised by the personal journey I had to travel. In advance a theme had been given to me, that of transformation, and also a text: 2 Corinthians 3.18 and 4.6. But it was only passing through the journey that revealed the meaning of the text and the theme, and gave me my *conférence* and my Easter morning sermon.

The overall context was an experience of genuine community in which was played out for me Jean Vanier's fundamental insight that the friendship of persons with profound disabilities can be deeply healing in itself. It felt a strangely 'given' experience. We were teamed up with a group from Nottingham – travelled with them, lived in the same hotel, and shared with them in those parts of the celebration which were undertaken in small communities rather than big crowds. We got to know some very remarkable people: like Jim and Patrick, Paddy and Brian, people who ran homes for those with learning disabilities in Nottingham and who, with headmaster Barry, were sources of endless fun, games and singing, as well as being totally unflappable with 28 pieces of luggage and half a dozen wheelchairs at the airport! There were parents with unforgettable courage in the face of bereavement and deterioration, and resilient young people, each of whom coped with 'minding' a far from easy character older than themselves.

But the outstanding experience was the friendship of the group members who were disabled: like Mervyn, who chattered non-stop, was full of questions and promised to pray for my Arthur; and Martin, whose face lit up with his wonderful, delightful smile as, holding my arm, he lurched and we both nearly fell over, or as he triumphantly placed his ironclad leg on an escalator; and David, who gently comforted tearful mothers after an emotional Good Friday prayer-time; and big Jonathan whose language consisted of 'Why?' and 'And me?', who needed someone's hand to hold but enjoyed running a race; and Paul, the gentle giant who mimed Jesus as with our little community we acted out an abbreviated Stations of the Cross on Good Friday. But, as we'll see later on, the most important friend, as far as I was concerned, was my namesake, Francis, a man with severe epilepsy and consequent brain damage. Together as a group we travelled and sang. Together we symbolically washed one another's feet. Together we had a riotous party with other groups in the neighbouring hotel on Maundy Thursday, learning new songs from the group from Gibraltar: 'Jesus is the Rock that rolls my blues away. He is the Rock that doesn't roll . . .' Together we walked with Christ to the cross, together we went to the Easter Fiesta, together in a crowd of 30,000 we joined a procession with the Blessed Sacrament and another singing 'Ave Maria' by torchlight after dark. That was the loving context in which I had to retread my personal calvary, so as to discern what Lourdes is really about and discover new depths of healing.

We arrived on Wednesday afternoon, and the first thing we two Methodists did was to visit the Grotto. For me it was disappointingly unspectacular as a cave – very ordinary, and too neatly paved and filled with flaunted religiosity. Eventually we followed around inside, feeling the wet rock, observing the spring under its glass, withdrawing in silence. But already I sensed that it was really about purification. As the days passed, I knew there was something deeply instinctive, indeed elemental, at work, not so much cure as the removal of stigma. The Lady told Bernadette that she was the Immaculate Conception, and that here was a place for sinners to find penitence, to wash and drink. The vision of Lourdes is the possibility of purity and holiness, getting rid of the stains and dirt that mark human life, being affirmed as acceptable and clean despite the mockery and rejection which is still the daily experience of people with learning disabilities in many parts of the world.

On Good Friday morning, Mervyn's mum was going to bathe in the spring water. I decided to go with her. We queued in silence. A little leaflet spoke of water as the sign of the love of Christ, the sign of our baptism, the sign of penance and purification, and my mind turned to the thought of dying with Christ that day to rise with him renewed. When we got inside the building, there were notices outside the cubicles in various languages, encouraging people to pray the Lord's Prayer. To my own considerable surprise, I found myself saying it in Greek, and having to stay with 'Thy will be done' as if passing through Gethsemane.

Once truly inside, with attendants all around and the need to follow the accepted ritual, I found it all rather distracting. After the feel of being wrapped in a cold, wet sheet, the rapid dip in the ice-cold water was exhilarating. No towels were provided since the lime-saturated water rapidly dries. I emerged disappointed that as I'd been lowered and raised by the attendants my face and hands had not entered the water. I knew I'd have to go to the taps and wash my face. But then there was no time. We had to meet our group to follow the Stations. I was to read the Scripture for the crucifixion scene. I'd chosen the Marcan version. We all mimed the hammering of the nails, and together we cried out with Jesus, 'My God, my God, why hast thou forsaken me?'

Later that day, after the massive crowds of the Good Friday service when I carried and held the cross, I escaped on my own, and took the steep path up the hill above the sacred area. There the most amazing series of sculptures, bronze and more than life-size, depict the Stations in full. It was a tough climb – not recommended for wheelchairs or people with disabilities . . . As I mounted I surprised myself as I began to be deeply moved and to weep at visual art in a way that only music, such as Bach's *St Matthew Passion*, had previously aroused in me. In identity with Mary I met my innocent suffering son and felt the pain of the sword piercing the mother's heart. With the women of Jerusalem I brought my child to the suffering, struggling Christ as he stumbled carrying the cross and begged a blessing. The tears streamed, and when I reached the top of the hill I couldn't gaze at the calvary. The afternoon sun was in my eyes, dazzling and blinding. Lining up the cross to cut the glare, all I could see were dark silhouettes. It was as though I were physically experiencing the paradox of Christ's exposure to the darkness of the world's sin and suffering which John's Gospel calls the hour of glory.

But then I followed the path around behind, and was amazed how, looking the other way having passed behind the cross, I saw the calvary illuminated, bright and clear – and the tears were dried and the sound of cowbells floated up from the meadow below. My eyes were opened to the grace which takes away the darkness, and peace began to dawn. Over the hill, cleverly placed before a natural fissure in the rock, there was the final scene, a group bringing the body to lay it in the tomb. I returned from my solitary struggle to community.

But the end was not yet. Good Friday evening, while meeting with a group of English speakers to meditate on suffering and to pray, to listen to testimonies, to sing the Taizé chant, 'Stay here, remain with me, watch and pray', like all the other mums in the place, not to mention some dads, I was again reduced to tears. It was that tough, and largely suppressed, place where I know that with the best intentions in the world, I've let Arthur down . . .

It was Francis who held my hand, and afterwards we went, just the two of us, to the Grotto. Francis was an old hand – he'd been to Lourdes eight times. Together we touched and kissed the wet rock, and I perceived something of the importance of that elemental touching – especially for people who find mental conception difficult. Together, we wondered in silence at the spring of pure water, and I acknowledged its beauty and mystery. Then we went to the taps, and Francis washed my face. My tears were purified. I washed his face, and together we cupped our hands and drank.

That Friday night in my weakness, I became convinced that I should be with my new friends in community for the Easter vigil – I hadn't the strength for ministry. But in the event circumstances demanded obedience, and on Holy Saturday ministry was required of me – the ministry of sharing, the ministry of praying, the ministry of speaking (the *conférence* for which I'd come), the ministry of sprinkling. So I found yet again that my healing came from obedience to that call. I could speak from a place of deep truth about transformation, and then on Easter Sunday proclaim a resurrection that makes a real difference to our lives.

> We all, with unveiled face, beholding/reflecting the glory of the Lord, are being changed into his likeness from one degree of glory to another . . . Therefore, having this ministry by the mercy of God, we do not lose heart . . . For what we preach is not ourselves, but Jesus Christ as Lord, with ourselves as your servants for Jesus' sake. For it is the God who said, 'Let light shine out of darkness,' who has shone in our hearts to give the light of knowledge of the glory of God in the face of Jesus Christ.
>
> (from 2 Cor. 3.18—4.6, RSV)

That first trip to Lourdes, then, had significant personal and ecumenical dimensions. Both were true too of my second pilgrimage ten years later, though very differently. The first had been so profoundly important that I knew I had to make sure I was not anticipating a replay; so I actually arranged to take Arthur with me. But I was also involved in a very different capacity – indeed, attempting to shape the ecumenical character of the pilgrimage as a member of the International Ecumenical Commission for Faith and Light. No way could the 2001 trip be a repeat of the earlier one.

Belonging to the International Ecumenical Commission was a wonderful experience. There were eight of us; in intention the group was made up of one lay and one ordained person from each of four churches: Roman Catholic, Eastern Orthodox, Anglican and Methodist. My Methodist colleague was a layman from Zimbabwe; the Anglicans were a priest from the UK and an American woman resident in Paris; the Orthodox were two women, one being from Moscow, the other a Syrian who'd been asked to represent a priest from Damascus as she was then working for the WCC in Geneva; the Catholics were a priest from Argentina and a woman from Northern Ireland, who was the convenor. It was truly international and ecumenical, yet meeting once a year for a few days together we became a very close fellowship of friends. Often we were welcomed at the original L'Arche communities in Trosly-Breuil or Cuise, each receiving hospitality from a foyer, so experiencing briefly the daily living together so characteristic of L'Arche, though sometimes struggling with language, tasting perhaps a little of the bafflement of a person with a learning disability. Once we met in Yorkshire, and once in Belfast, where we visited the recently formed L'Arche community, which paradoxically was finding itself relating better to Protestants than Catholics.

As the pilgrimage approached we were given the task of working to make it as ecumenical as possible. It was not at all easy. We came up with ideas and plans, but then others had controlling stakes, not least the Lourdes priests. Along with the overall organizer of the pilgrimage I found myself making trips to Paris to meet the Lourdes representative – that certainly challenged my French! But overall I fear there was less ecumenical participation then than ten years before, and as Faith and Light became ever more ecumenical in many parts of the world, this may have been a factor contributing to debates as to whether or not in future Lourdes pilgrimages should be replaced with more regional gatherings appropriate to the membership. Gradually it also became apparent that the International Ecumenical Commission had little real impact on the organization because it was not directly plugged into the leadership. As an expensive luxury it was eventually discontinued, but some of those friendships have been long-lasting.

Meanwhile, for Easter 2001 I had a variety of responsibilities in Lourdes, and also found myself ministering to others in many little ways – Protestants feeling disoriented, parents with questions. I knew in advance that I'd not be able to devote myself to coping with Arthur, yet wanted to take him. Happily the solution was straightforward – one of the students who'd cared for him at home and taken him on holiday with the Catholic Handicapped Children's Fellowship was an old hand at Lourdes, a regular helper with pilgrimages for children with disabilities from the UK. James travelled out with us and shared a bedroom with Arthur, becoming his principal carer; then he stayed on for his own regular pilgrimage the following week.

So for that one and only time Arthur had a passport and went abroad. The charter flight to Tarbes went from Manchester; so Peter and Mary Humble kindly helped us catch the flight by putting us up overnight. Then there was a coach ride. In neither case could Arthur sit in his special wheelchair, which had to be taken apart and folded to go in the hold, then reassembled. Arthur had to be carried on and off each form of transport, and for the long waits he needed his beanbag to relax on. I could never have coped with it all without James' help. It was in the coach that I noticed the extraordinary thing that was happening: Arthur was exceptionally alert, looking around at everything, stimulated by these new experiences. This was an Arthur not really seen before, or indeed since. Apart from some restful times sunbathing on the hotel roof, with Arthur on his beanbag in the shade, I have strong memories of how this alertness and engagement persisted through the days of the pilgrimage, how he ate with enthusiasm, how he vocalized and smiled.

And there were three special moments:

1 Maundy Thursday's foot-washing was shared in small groups in the hotels. I shall never forget Arthur's start of surprise as he felt the water on his foot – it broke the silence, but with that and his giggle, he brought the whole group together.

2 Jean Vanier found a moment to visit our hotel early one morning. Arthur was still in bed, but their gentle first meeting was something very special, for James as well as myself.

3 The crowds pouring into the basilica for one of the great liturgies were overwhelming, and Arthur in his chair was almost submerged by all the people around. A small group of us headed for the exit, and gradually escaped. A substitute for participation was particularly lovely: in the open air and the twilight we gathered by the statue of Bernadette, and the majority being Catholics, we together worked through the rosary – a new ecumenical experience for some, including myself. With Arthur and others who had disabilities an amazing peace and quiet joy seemed to hold us together in Christ.

L'Arche

These two trips to Lourdes with Faith and Light, ten years apart, bracketed important involvements in L'Arche. It was in 1993 that I first visited the original L'Arche community at Trosly-Breuil. I had met Jean somewhere in East Anglia at a retreat for long-term assistants in L'Arche. One mealtime he sat with me and Donald Allchin, all three of us there as contributors to the programme, and asked us if we could get together a group of theologians to meet at Trosly-Breuil to reflect on the significance of L'Arche. Thus began a series of profoundly important gatherings. The fruits of the first two meetings I was able to edit and publish in the book, *Encounter with Mystery*. Later some larger meetings included long-term leaders in L'Arche and people from other Christian communities, such as Corrymeela and Iona. Reflection began to stimulate all participants to deeper theological engagement both with disability and with community.

At the end of the first meeting Jean led us in a process of collecting together significant 'sayings' from our days of conversation. It was a bit like creating our own 'wisdom-book', similar to the books of Proverbs and Ecclesiastes in the Bible. Here is the list published in *Encounter with Mystery*:

> Community means you never suffer alone.
> Brokenness is one of God's greatest gifts; it is the key to accepting human brokenness and the brokenness of the Church.
> What is really human is the capacity to ask for help, and that is the gift of the unlikely givers.
> *Moi tout seule ne pas capable.* (Me alone can't do it.)
> I smile. Therefore you are.
> I need to be loved by somebody with skin on.
> The greatest problem is when people behave as if you are not there.
> This is a privileged desert.
> They [persons with mental disabilities, the poor] have the capacity to evangelize us [the intelligent, priests, etc.].
> My saviour is the one who needs me.
> In creation there is fragility and vulnerability: that is the nature of creation.
> We need the stranger; we lack the very people we are afraid of because they are different.
> Christian faith is not problem-solving but mystery-encountering.

That list encompasses many of the profound insights emerging, and foreshadowed deep shifts in my own thinking, which was more than once opened up by the challenge of preparing contributions for these meetings. We were 'putting the mind into the heart', and vice versa.

One such development was recognition of the vocation of persons with learning disabilities. For me it signalled the important point that Arthur would not simply be part of *my* ministry, but had a significance of his own (see Chapter 7). Jean describes a young assistant in L'Arche saying:

> I come from a competitive and conflict-ridden world. I was taught to hide my weaknesses and limits behind a mask, and to be strong and aggressive in order to win in studies, work and sport . . . Antonio is leading me into another world, a world of love and tenderness, where we respect one another, need one another, live in communion, one with another; a world where we try to help each other to use gifts to grow humanly and spiritually . . .

So, wrote Jean:

> living with Antonio, feeding him and bathing his fragile body day after day, clothing him in his littleness, helplessness and trust, calls forth qualities in the heart of others. Listening to his non-verbal language, and trying to understand his pain and needs, helps people lower their barriers and calls them into a communion of the heart which has a transforming effect.

They have the capacity to evangelize us.

Yet some participants were very unhappy about this differentiation between 'us' and 'them'. They felt profoundly the sense of identification I'd glimpsed in the chapel at Monyhull Hospital. The differences were submerged in the revelation of our common vulnerability, our basic human fragility, our fundamental need for one another. But reducing all to the same common denominator is not necessarily the most creative approach. Not for nothing was I challenged to produce a piece on 'Welcoming difference'. It is the encounter with 'otherness' in the person with learning disabilities which enables the transformation experienced by L'Arche assistants. So, paradoxically, naming the 'otherness' of the 'other' may be the prerequisite for reciprocity, as well as making it possible to articulate the way in which 'competent us' are ministered to by those we thought we were there to help and assist. Somehow we needed to hold together both insights – our identity and our difference.

Which led on to the recognition that in community there is a profound mutuality. This is not top-down charity, because those who imagine they go to help find they receive more than they give. Occasionally this crucial insight would get overlaid by a rather patronizing Catholic sentimentality about the 'poor', of which I found myself personally very critical; it seemed to gloss over the realities of disability, with all its pain and heartache. Yet it certainly contributed to another significant point. In Christian tradition religious communities have been categorized as 'active' or 'contemplative', but L'Arche turns out to be both: the people who commit themselves to living in community with persons who have learning disabilities appear to be doing good, entering as it were an 'active' order, but what they discover is a form of 'contemplative' life as they learn to 'wait', to pay attention to slow or non-verbal communication, to discern a 'presence' in those they seek to serve, to discover the sacramental dimension of bodies. It's no accident that washing one another's feet has become a significant liturgical act in both L'Arche and Faith and Light. Partly it's that this enables communion without the ecumenical challenges presented by sharing Eucharist, but it's more than that. 'Washing and cleansing those who cannot perform these functions for themselves are a basic part of daily life in the communities', and 'washing the body when it is broken or in pain is an essential way of caring for the person.'[3] So ordinary routine becomes sacred as this daily necessity is made sacramental, an expression of the communion of the community gathered around human bodiliness and brokenness – indeed, the bodiliness and brokenness of Christ.

But the significance of these meetings for me lay not just in the conversation and the articulation of insights, but in invitations to share evenings with core members and assistants in the foyers at Trosly-Breuil. More than once I was sent to join for their evening meal and prayers the residents of La Forestière, the foyer specially built to accommodate those with the most severe disabilities. It was here that two experiences occurred of profound moment.

The first centred on a man with Down's syndrome, whose name, significantly, was Christophe – Christ-bearer. He simply squatted at my feet, rested his chin on arms folded across my knees and gazed into my face – a gaze mutually held for ages. To understand why this was so deeply transforming we must scroll back to Lourdes on that Good Friday evening in 1991. The incident that triggered my tears and the loving response of my namesake Francis was this. A man with Down's syndrome was giving testimony at great length. Someone eventually suggested, with great respect and gentleness, that he should wind it up. He replied that he had to say one more thing – what a wonderful mother he had! Afterwards the colleague who accompanied me to Lourdes said, 'I suppose Arthur will never be able to say that to you', and I realized with sorrow how little real response he was then able to give me – we barely had eye contact, and often he pushed me away, hating to be handled. From Christophe I somehow received the affirmation I needed as Arthur's mother.

The second centred on Edith. I was again at La Forestière for a meal and I found myself sitting right opposite her. To my shame, I felt disgusted by her slobbering her food, the red wine she clearly loved splattered all over the napkin round her neck. I was deeply chastened by my reaction – perhaps I was meant to see how people sometimes felt at table with my son. Sometime later, on another visit, I sat next to Edith on a sofa after the meal, gently trying to restrain her self-abuse as she repeatedly banged her head with her fist. I once heard Jean Vanier say that Mother Teresa used to speak of 'repulsion, compassion, then wonderment': I'd been through the repulsion, I'd reached compassion – the wonderment was still to come. Next time I visited, Edith had just died. I joined the wake where person after person gave testimony to what Edith had meant to them – it challenged my French, but was somehow all the more powerful for being only half-understood. Afterwards a small group of us visitors went with Jean to see Edith laid out in the little chapel at the foyer, surrounded by flowers and candles, still and at peace, quite beautiful. We simply gazed in wonderment.

I have continued to value not only opportunities to visit L'Arche communities in various places – Northern Ireland, Canada and the USA, besides France – but also invitations to contribute as a theologian to workshops and retreats. It's been a particular privilege for me, with my friend and former colleague David Ford, to meet regularly with Jean and the international coordinators, Christine and Jean-Christophe, during their tenure of office. As with Faith and Light, so with L'Arche I've found fellowship and friendship; yet only once with each organization has Arthur been involved: neither organization has a presence in the UK West Midlands, so local participation has been denied us. Arthur met Faith and Light in Lourdes; he met L'Arche in Canterbury, again on pilgrimage.

It all came about because Jean asked David Ford and myself to address L'Arche's IGA (International General Assembly), which in 2002 met at Swanwick. Immediately afterwards the participants were to go on a pilgrimage to Canterbury, and everyone begged us to join them, and bring Arthur. Somehow, at the last minute, the organizers arranged for a proper bed and other necessities to make it possible. I returned home to pick up the car and Arthur, breaking the long journey for a few hours at David's home in Cambridge. From there Daniel, David's son and my godson, joined us and the four of us travelled together. After a reflective foot-washing in the crypt of the cathedral, the joyous gathering in Canterbury turned into a party for Arthur's thirty-fifth birthday! The night was to be spent camping out together in a sports hall. Everyone except Arthur slept on the floor, and by the time I'd got him changed and ready for bed, many were turning in. But Arthur was so excited by it all, not least the echoing hall, that he kept craning up, shouting out his range of 'words' and happy noises at high volume. My heart sank – would anyone get any sleep? As soon as the light was turned out, though, Arthur put his head down on the pillow and sleep rapidly overtook him. What a relief!

Faith and Light again

A few months later I was at Faith and Light's IGA, which took place at a conference centre near the Pope's summer residence outside Rome. I'd been asked to address the assembly, with time enough to share not only some ideas developed in conversation with L'Arche but also my personal journey with Mary, the mother of Jesus. I told the story of how when Arthur was a teenager we'd been invited to that carol service at the local convent, and I'd become deeply conscious of the huge statue of Mary towering over me in the chapel; I shared that prayer-poem which had formed in my mind by the time I'd pushed the buggy back up the block (see Chapter 2). I explained how it played a crucial role in enabling me to accept my own brokenness as a mother. The *pietà* had become a healing presence, as exemplar, as image and 'type' of the suffering of women down the centuries – for women have so often suffered through their sons and their husbands, lost in violence or war, lost at sea or down mines, lost or maimed . . . On holiday in Brittany I'd been captured by the great carved calvaries depicting Mary with the women at the deposition of Christ's body. I was intrigued by Simeon's words to Mary in the Temple: 'Behold, this child is set for the fall and rising of many in Israel, and for a sign that is spoken against (and a sword will pierce through your own soul also) . . .' Mary's pierced heart was implicated in the Passion. I then told how this unexpected journeying with

Mary became a literal journey in 1991 when Jean Vanier invited me to join the Faith and Light anniversary pilgrimage to Lourdes. For the Lourdes story is of Bernadette, a simple local girl – indeed, maybe she was a person with slight learning disabilities – and of how she met with Our Lady more than once, was shown a new spring of water, and heard the Lady say that she was the Immaculate Conception, and that here was a place for sinners to find penitence, to wash and drink. So I discovered that Lourdes is primarily about purification, about the removal of stigma, about holy waters bringing atonement and absolution, and I described how through those days I'd experienced inner healing, purification and reconciliation as I re-trod my own path in Mary's company. I guess some traditional Roman Catholics and Eastern Orthodox found my take on Mary a bit surprising, yet it was obviously telling for parents with challenges similar to mine.

This meeting had other dimensions, too. I vividly remember the depth of fellowship in the sharing-group to which I was assigned – strangers thrown together from across the world finding they truly belonged to one another because of their common experience. Someone from Australia led the group and gave each of us a beautifully carved and polished wooden 'holding cross'; it still lies under my pillow, and fits into my palm as I try to focus prayer. Here the International Ecumenical Commission did make a contribution to planning ecumenical worship, and it was my privilege to preside at a Methodist Communion service. And here I was introduced to the delegation from Russia by Natasha, my colleague in the International Commission. Little did I know that soon I'd be with them in Moscow.

In 2003, I was resident in Moscow to teach a three-week module for the United Methodist seminary. It was an amazing experience altogether, but most of all for the two Sunday afternoons spent with Faith and Light groups, gathered around icons, but with the same simple faith-sharing that I'd found wherever Faith and Light or L'Arche groups meet together. I shall never forget going out for a walk while the communal meal was prepared. We went to the Parc Kulturi, where all the old statues of Lenin and Stalin are stored alongside other sculptures. On each arm I had a man with learning disabilities and no language – so my lack of Russian was irrelevant, and there was a real sense of togetherness as we walked. Every so often I'd be pulled over to stroke the head of a carved lion. It all seemed a bit surreal, very moving, miraculously unexpected. Talking of the unexpected – at the end of my stay, I was about to leave, waiting for a taxi with the Seminary's secretary, when a car screamed to a halt and out stepped one of the local Faith and Light leaders with Jean Vanier – our visits had almost overlapped!

Seven years later, in 2010, I again went to Moscow, this time at the invitation of Faith and Light, to join the celebration of their twentieth anniversary. That was another remarkable experience, a big five-day gathering at a rundown Soviet workers' holiday complex in the countryside outside Moscow. The very diverse cross-section of age groups and competences – persons with disabilities, parents, friends, grandmothers, families with babies and toddlers – all making their own contribution, was in itself a parable of the theme: 'Everyone counts and matters for the whole "body"'. Such talented people, too – with visual displays and backdrops, drama and beautiful icons, not to mention the music, that wonderful mixture of the songs, Taizé chants and choruses characteristic of Faith and Light everywhere, together with Orthodox prayers and chants. The question I was asked most often was whether they were like other Faith and Light groups. What was so lovely to my mind was the way in which they had 'encultured' into an Orthodox environment the features of Faith and Light tradition that enabled simple and inclusive sharing, caring and praying. One particular icon was everywhere: the ancient Coptic depiction of Jesus with his arm round his friend, the martyr-saint Menas. I asked if I might take a copy back and was told, 'Of course. We just print them off the Internet and stick them on cardboard.' So now Jesus and St Menas sit beside my bed, and I can feel Jesus' hand of friendship on my shoulder whenever I turn to the icon.

As their special guest I had to address the opening gathering. Every session was based on colour and light, sound and music, welcome and smiles. So it was easy to share pictures of Arthur, explain why he and everyone else counts, and matters for the whole 'body', by reflecting on 1 Corinthians 12, and teaching an English action song – 'Heads, shoulders, knees and toes'. That was a stroke of genius – people kept doing it all through those five days! In the two sessions I had with parents, we gradually found more and more that we shared – our feelings and questions, struggles and joys, despite the necessary mediation of the translator (we were mostly mothers and he was a man!). People slowly began to talk, and afterwards, some came to me to share their special problems and concerns. I found myself drawing on the experience of many years with Arthur and the ways in which New Testament passages had spoken to my needs and cries, as well as the resources of recent journeys and reflections – especially a recent trek up Sinai and its special message to me that you go on pilgrimage to find God at home, in the sacrament of the present moment, in the struggles as well as the smiles. Talking of smiles, that was one of the most striking things as I watched people arriving and greeting one another. Indeed, my lack of Russian meant I spent a lot of time just watching, sensing the sheer warmth and support and fun going on. And there was space for walking and reflection, once the rain stopped – I discovered the lake, and the forest, and the wildflowers and the mosquitoes! True, the sports facilities and gardens were rundown and going wild, but wilderness has its own sacredness and is a good place to be alone, without being lonely. And the setting became all the more important for the celebration day on Saturday when the weather was kind – from the liturgies through to the evening 'pilgrimage', the party and the bonfire, everything was simply joyous. This event produced its own poem:

> I think, and therefore I am:
> In the deep, dark well of an inturned self,
> Where echoes are hollow,
> Existence is burden.
>
> You smile, and therefore I am:
> In the lightening sky of the dawning day,
> Attention grasped
> By being that's other,
> Existence is birdsong.
>
> I smile, and therefore you are:
> In the afternoon, in communion, we
> Together smile.
> And all's worthwhile.
> The rainbow beauty of smiles through cheerfulness
> Can focus flickering flames of hopefulness,
> Despite the gathering evening shades.
> With sparks of light
> At dead of night,
> Existence is bonfire!

I came away from this celebration deeply humbled by the courage of women on their own, with their disabled child now adult and no support services. By comparison, my life has been cushioned at the practical level, freed to make so many journeys by my husband's commitment to Arthur, blessed by contacts with so many remarkable people, privileged as minister and theologian to reflect and articulate responses from Scripture and experience to life's challenges. Some of the theological fruits will be shared in the following chapters, as we turn from narrative to consider what I've learned about creation and the cross largely through Arthur and others like him.

4

Creation

————◆◆◆————

In creation there is fragility and vulnerability; that is the nature of creation.

That was one of the wise sayings collected at our first L'Arche meeting. My original anguished question had been, 'How can I go on believing in a good Creator God when something so drastic has gone wrong with the creation of a new human being?' Meanwhile, acceptance of Arthur's condition as an accident was a reminder that we're all vulnerable, all accident-prone, that creation is fragile, that loss and death are inherently part of the life we know on earth. This was reinforced by the experience of identifying with persons who are impaired for life, an identification acknowledged by assistants in L'Arche and felt by myself in worship at Monyhull Hospital. So the questions shifted: What does it mean to be human? How are we to make sense of creation's fragility? What does our vulnerability mean for understanding God's creative purposes? This is one of the areas where now I would claim that Arthur has given me privileged access to the deepest truths of Christianity.

Creatureliness

Come with me in imagination on a visit to Africa. Our African guide walks in front through the bush. Suddenly he stops and urges us back. After a bit we turn and ask, 'What's the problem?' He points to some waving branches: elephant! We've been dangerously close. We set out downwind and give it a wide berth. We never saw the beast, until later, back in our camp, we see an elephant splash across the channel of water. All night the call of the nightjar, the bark of hyena, the sound of roaring lion. Next morning early we walk miles through the bush tracking lion, but the cats are elusive. We find fresh elephant

71

dung, and nervously take a circular route back. And the next 24 hours are the same. We hear hippo grunting and our guide poles the dugout away fast in the other direction. In the distance we see buffalo grazing and avoid the area. We go in search of the leopard we've been hearing, but see nothing but wildebeest and leaping buck, lechwe and impala. We were camping and walking in the Okavango Delta, one of the last places in Africa where you can still have experiences similar to the old explorers. Our guide had an ancient spear and a knife, but for safety we were really dependent upon traditional skills – tracking, observation, caution, keeping the fire alight all night. We didn't see much game, but slid through long grassy meadows in the punt on a level with frogs and dragonflies, spiders' webs and waterlilies. It was a rich paradise. Yet always the *frisson* of the wild, the edge of insecurity . . .

This was an experience of being human in the natural context of creation, an experience Westerners now rarely have. We were little and vulnerable in a stunningly beautiful but potentially threatening world. The skills of survival were those we've long lost. There was something awesome about just being there. Yet even so we were cushioned compared with our hunter-gatherer ancestors: we had tinned food and tin-openers, we had insect repellent and Anthisan. We escaped the dreaded malaria and sleeping-sickness, but on our return appreciated the benefit of antibiotics to deal with our tick typhus. And we would escape, flying dramatically over the swamp and seeing the giraffe far below . . . Nevertheless I believe we had a salutary reminder of how artificial our lives have become, and what the human condition really is in the context of creation. We are creatures alongside other creatures.

So what makes us human as distinct from other creatures? This is an age-old question. The Greek philosopher Aristotle famously said: 'Man [using the Greek word which means any member of the human species] is a rational animal', and certainly our large brains have enabled humankind to take over the earth. Our upright stance and dextrous hands, the ability to use tools, laughter, language and various other features have figured in discussion over centuries, though it's been pointed out that someone could have all these competences, but if they lacked normal human affections they'd be considered inhuman.[4] In any case, scientific research has shown that pretty well every one of these features have precursors among birds and animals, and this is true too of things like complex social organization and even empathy with close kin. Life is truly a continuum and we share 98.6 per cent of our DNA with chimpanzees. Popular science books and TV programmes show that by taking this continuum seriously we can learn a lot about ourselves, but we can also begin to identify key features which do make a difference.

The human species is born premature, underdeveloped and utterly dependent. Our full development depends on interaction with others, on slow incorporation into community and culture through a learning process, which begins with smiling and the nonsense-language that mothers coo over their babies as they caress them. Those big brains, it seems, developed in order to handle the complexity of our social relationships, with laughter, music and religion all stimulating body chemistry which facilitates community, while our capacity to mind-read and make moral judgements surpasses anything found in other species. Human children share the rewards of cooperation and have a strong sense of fairness; chimps may collaborate but each will grab what they can get out of it. Chimps have close social bonds but only with near relatives – with strangers they're violent and intensely suspicious; whereas we deal with strangers every time we go to a supermarket. Human beings cooperate with unrelated others, share tasks across complex social organizations, trade with others and make deals which depend on trust. Within the natural world our capacity to trust unrelated strangers is truly remarkable.[5]

These observations constitute quite a shift in perspective. It's long been assumed that competition and the 'survival of the fittest' are features characteristic of the natural world, and so of humans too. Of course, there's plenty of evidence to suggest exactly that: violence and war seem intractable realities throughout human history; competitive individualism is endemic in our culture. It seems unnatural for human beings to welcome those who are different. Once I was driving Arthur through some lanes just outside our home city of Birmingham. At one point we came round a corner to see a horse straining at the reins as the dismounted rider tried to steer it reluctantly along the road. I stopped the car and we waited. As they went past, the girl said, 'She can't stand the Shetlands.' It took me a moment to realize what she meant. Over the hedge in the field were several tiny little shaggy Shetland ponies. It seemed that the horse recognized that they were the same but different, and so scary and threatening. When asked to speak about 'welcoming difference' for L'Arche I began with that story, suggesting it was a parable of how human beings tend to react to one another.

Throughout history, race, ethnicity and other differences have generated reaction against people seen as alien, strange, threateningly different – yet the same. The period of the slave trade, I discovered, generated a sense of the European having a dark twin, the African, and needing to subjugate, even kill this challenging double. Religious differences have compounded reaction against 'the other', and paradoxically the bitterest conflicts are often between those who are most alike: Jews, Christians and Muslims share a common history and heritage, but Christians are blamed by Jews for the Holocaust and by Muslims for the Crusades. It seems as if the more alike we are, the less able we are to welcome difference. Yet over the millennia humankind has also developed the ability to extend the empathy and social bonds characteristic of kith and kin to wider human networks, and even to the human race as a whole. We are torn between our propensity for suspicion and violence, and our miraculous capacity to cross boundaries and transcend those natural tendencies.

What then is the human condition? The classic modern question has been 'Apes or angels? Creation or evolution?' After more than 100 years that debate is still in the air. And isn't it a great irony that since Darwin reduced the human species to monkeys, we human beings have gone so far over the top we've virtually destroyed the planet and come almost to the brink of wiping ourselves out? Since we stopped daring to think we're angels, we've turned ourselves into God – sure we're autonomous, responsible only to our own individual sense of what is right and true. Maybe, like post-modern architects, we need to rediscover classical perspectives, the wisdom of the past. So let's direct our gaze back, to ancient philosophies, ancient answers to the haunting question, 'What are we, the human species?'

It's a pity that, in the debates about evolution, people have forgotten this biblical passage from Ecclesiastes 3.18–21:

> I said in my heart with regard to human beings that God is testing them to show that they are but animals. For the fate of humans and the fate of animals is the same; as one dies, so dies the other. They all have the same breath, and humans have no advantage over the animals; for all is vanity. All go to one place; all are from the dust, and all turn to dust again. Who knows whether the human spirit goes upwards and the spirit of animals goes downwards to the earth?

Long before Darwin, it was recognized that human beings are part of the created order. Such a recognition enables us to rediscover better perspective on ourselves and our life: whether as a whole or in particular (an elephant, for example, or a tree), nature is so much bigger, older, younger, than 'me'. Fragility and vulnerability are characteristic of all creation and, of all species, the naked human is one of the most fragile and vulnerable. Yet we've learned to cut down trees and poach elephants for their ivory. A placard at the entry to the Wildfowl and Wetlands Trust at Slimbridge in Gloucestershire used to proclaim: 'Humanity is the most aggressive and destructive species on earth.'

In Genesis 1, humanity is made king of creation, the one to 'have dominion over' the fish of the sea, the birds of air, cattle, the wild animals of earth. This translation no doubt encouraged the explorers and exploiters of the early modern period, but in the ancient world a king was the protector of his people, and the Hebrew verb translated 'have dominion' actually means 'shepherding'. Domination is a distortion. Yet ancient wisdom did recognize that humankind was creation's crown. The fourth-century bishop Gregory of Nyssa suggested that humanity was made in God's image to be king of creation, but being both physical and spiritual had the choice to live like animals or live like angels. Rationality meant not the kind of aggressive dominance modernity has made it, but an opportunity to stretch the mind, discipline the self, for union with God, to collaborate with God as God's image and representative in the created order, tending God's garden. It's a pity that it's taken doom-watchers to remind us that an ecological perspective is what the wisdom of our tradition has always encouraged. We are part of the natural order, and the whole natural order is threatened when we cease to respect our place there, when we forget our fragility, littleness, weakness, in our desire to master rather than shepherd.

This sense of who we really are challenges many unquestioned assumptions: the success-values of our culture, our attitudes to suffering, struggle and failure, our expectations of perfection. Let's get back to the perspective of hunter-gatherers in the African bush and ask ourselves what would be success in that context. Isn't success an irrelevant category? In such a context people need survival skills to negotiate the challenges, alertness to the world round about, mutual support in the face of a potentially hostile environment, and the ability to collaborate across natural divides. What's important is not success but a sense of being part of something bigger than oneself, a willingness to give way to the greater good of the community, awareness of one's creatureliness and vulnerability, a response of awe, humility, wonder at the beauty of it all. You can see why poets and prophets were honoured for their capacity to weave stories that give hope, point beyond the immediacy of current dangers and express the community's sense of wonder and identity. You can see why religion and worship emerged among early humans, why fear and trust, obedience and respect lie at the heart of religion.

Persons limited in their capacity by impairments not only reinforce this insight into the way we're part of the natural order and therefore subject to its vulnerabilities, but also enable a shift in values, away from individualism, dominance, competitiveness, to community, mutuality – a human ecology which has the potential to be 'angelic'. In his book *Dependent Rational Animals* the philosopher Alasdair MacIntyre brings together two questions: 'Why is it important for us to attend to, and to understand, what human beings have in common with members of other intelligent animal species?' and 'What makes attention to human vulnerability and disability important for moral philosophers?' He recognizes that these questions bear fundamentally on the matter of human virtue. Persons as damaged as Arthur lack the very characteristics we've highlighted as human – language, intelligence, the ability to read other minds, a moral sense; yet like any other baby the first thing Arthur did was to smile, and in their own way persons with learning disabilities are often more trusting, more mature in relationships, than the rest of us, able to call forth those characteristically human qualities of response to one another – indeed the true human values that Paul calls the gifts of the Spirit: love, joy, peace, patience, kindness, goodness, faithfulness, gentleness and self-control (Gal. 5.22). Indeed, that some persons lack moral autonomy surely highlights the point that true human goodness is never individualistic – it's corporate, something found in community.

In the spirituality of L'Arche God's presence is found in the everyday experience of sharing life with those who have learning disabilities, the most vulnerable persons on earth. The L'Arche insight that what really makes us human is the capacity to ask for help challenges modern claims to autonomy. It also challenges our individualism and success-values. We need to learn to wash one another's feet.

Modernity and the question of God

'Mankind come of age' was the striking phrase with which the theologian Dietrich Bonhoeffer characterized modernity. Modern man had reached a kind of maturity which encouraged superiority *vis-à-vis* the past, especially when it came to what most regarded as superstitious religious fears. At the heart of it was the sense of human autonomy:

- a growing out of dependence on supernatural powers
- being in control
- mastery of the once hostile environment
- scientific progress, especially medical breakthroughs
- industrial development
- liberty and equality
- independence and democracy
- human beings in charge of their own destiny – making their own moral choices rather than kowtowing to authorities whether human or divine.

Modernity left no room for God.

The modern (post-Enlightenment) account of the human condition was optimistic and humanistic. True for 100 years and more, it tended to apply only to educated males of a certain social class – but now all kinds of people have claimed the same rights in our post-industrial, post-colonial, post-feminist world. And the idea that if we could only get the right formula the whole world would be put to rights has come to pervade the popular mind, encouraged by a press that deplores anything going wrong and seeks to apportion blame for every accident. Post-modernity has not shifted our assumption that life is meant to be perfect and, because we suppose life is meant to be perfect, the biggest problem for religious belief remains the issue of arbitrary suffering. For life obviously isn't perfect, and the abiding impact of modernity is disclosed by our anxiety about this.

One thing that strikes me as I read Christian writings from past centuries is the lack of concern with this problem. Ordinary people in earlier centuries also suffered. Indeed, high infant mortality, brief life expectancy, inability to alleviate many medical conditions, epidemics and unrelieved famine meant that they suffered far more than most people who are now troubled by the question. Once there seems to have been more general acceptance of suffering, and indeed death,

77

as a natural part of human life. This contrast between modernity and the past is striking. Why was the atheist critique not so powerful in past centuries? At least part of the answer lies in the reality of living precariously, close to creation, which was as awe-inspiring as it was sustaining. And not just in Africa: the fear of the wolf haunts European legend and literature. People knew they were small and vulnerable; they depended on God and at the same time feared the unknown mysterious power at the heart of all things. They didn't think to question its existence or goodness if life turned rough – rather they examined their own hearts and lives to see how they had offended.

Earlier generations, then, accepted the creatureliness of the human condition – vulnerable, mortal – and were concerned with finding the wisdom to face and cope with the hardships of life; moderns have been offended by them. Put yourself back in the bush: you don't question the right of the elephant to charge or the lion to pounce on its prey. The world you inhabit is not something over which you have control: we had to sign an indemnity before setting off – for there things could happen for which the organization could not be held in any way responsible. Meanwhile, in safety-conscious Britain the dramatic Symonds Yat of my youth has been tamed by building a wall round it!

Given that much past suffering is now removable, modern anxiety about this problem may seem the more ironic. Indeed, that anxiety seems generated by dramatically improved expectations. Most people in the West are protected from the sense of life's precariousness with which all previous generations have had to reckon. A century ago people had large families because not all would survive into adulthood. Serious poverty was endemic, hygiene barely understood and health insecure: death happened in the midst of life. Westerners now expect children to be born healthy and to surmount childhood illnesses through vaccination or antibiotics. Death even in old age is sterilized in hospitals. The result is that when things are not perfect, people react with horror. They cry out for better safety precautions and demand the development of miracle cures. If they believe in God, they expect miraculous answers to prayer.

So God is supposed to have the power to wave a magic wand and put things right. But what would power be in the context of the African bush? Wouldn't any power which took control of that environment in fact destroy it? If it is to be what it is, it has to be let be. Absolute power corrupts absolutely. Maybe a daring thought, but God's absolute power – omnipotence – might be demonic. Indeed, in the modern period some have argued that God does not exist, others that, supposing there is a God, God must be a demon. The notion of a good Creator has become problematic in general – no wonder it preoccupied me for so many years. Maybe it's because we've destroyed the wilderness and created our own comfort zones that the problem arises. We've failed to realize that taking control of the environment destroys its ecology and upsets its balance. We've failed to notice that in creation things are not organized solely for our benefit, and from our point of view natural processes are profoundly ambiguous: good consequences deeply intertwined with bad. For example, life probably began in deep ocean vents associated with the volcanic activity which also produces tsunamis; and it is the fact of mutation that allowed our very evolution, along with genetic diseases and chromosomal abnormalities like Down's syndrome. As the Bible puts it, 'All flesh is grass, and all the goodliness thereof is as the flower of the field: The grass withereth, the flower fadeth . . .' (Isa. 40.6–8, AV). Not only is human existence deeply integrated with the complexity, mutability and vulnerability of the whole creation, but the whole nature of the created order would be profoundly different if it were rearranged to suit us.

Yet even more fundamental than our distancing from the wilderness is the loss of the right context for thinking about God. Surely for Christians, thinking about God should begin not with the projection on to the heavens of the most powerful agent we can imagine – a male fixer, with absolute power – but with Jesus. The extraordinary heart of the gospel lies in God's acceptance of limitation, the self-emptying seen in the Incarnation. It was the twentieth-century 'mystic' Simone Weil who opened my eyes to the relevance of this to creation. 'The Creation is an abandonment,' she wrote.[6] 'Creation is abdication . . . God has emptied himself.' 'The apparent absence of God in this world is the actual reality of God,' she said. What she meant was that if the eternal, infinite God were to create something other than the divine self, it would be necessary for God to 'withdraw', allowing 'space', as it were, for something other than God to be. Of course, at this point we're struggling to speak of what we cannot know in inadequate and limited human terms, using a kind of picture language, but it's the best we can do. Another inadequate image might be that of a loving parent letting the child be, allowing the child to take risks so as to mature and become herself. There is love and self-emptying involved.

It's interesting that Simone Weil pursued the potential coherence between creation and cross: 'Not only the Passion but the Creation itself is a renunciation and sacrifice on the part of God.' Jesus cries out, 'My God, my God, why hast thou forsaken me?' and Godforsakenness constitutes the creature's existence and freedom to be itself. 'If God did not abandon them they would not exist. His presence would annul their existence as a flame kills a butterfly.'

'He's got the whole world in his hands,' we sing, yet it's like trying to hold a butterfly – God contains but does not constrain, for fear of damaging. As I indicated just now, to try to grasp what God is like we have to use picture language, for in principle God is not like anything created. God is utterly 'other' than anything we limited creatures can conceive, and the only way to get a glimmering is to set different, sometimes even contradictory, images side by side, for any single image taken literally is an idol. Yet contemplation of aspects of our lives or of creation can lead to insight, and insights are sometimes best expressed in poetry, for we know poetic images are not meant to be taken literally. Let me share two of my own poems.

The circumstances of the first came directly out of noticing something about Arthur, namely his uncanny likeness to my father once he'd grown a moustache (see Chapter 1). Yet no two persons could have been less alike: my father, a distinguished and rather awe-inspiring headmaster with a massive intellect, and Arthur with his tiny head and small brain. It led to reflections on the likeness and unlikeness involved in the Bible's suggestion that human beings are made in God's image (Gen. 1.26–27), and Jesus Christ is 'the image of the invisible God' (Col. 1.15).

Elusive Likeness

A glimpse of an image is caught
in an almost ginger moustache
and a certain look round the eyes.
With its littleness and loss
of brain development
the grandson's likeness belies
the grandfather's dignity
and impressive intellect –
an offence one might surmise.
Yet the glint of a loving smile

encaptures its genesis
in shy, suggestive guise.

So the human likeness to God:
a gargoyle one might surmise,
a mirror-image that lies,
its hazy reflections reversed –
huge hints, yet hard to trace,
that veil their archetype,
yet focused face to face
reveal what love implies.

So too God's image in Christ:
God's likeness in human guise –
an unlike likeness formed
from utter otherness
in close proximity;
transcendent holiness
in physicality;
in littleness and loss
an outline sketch that tries
to capture its genesis
in that look about the eyes;
intangible, infinite grace
extended in tender touch
and shining from the face –
invisible visage caught
in expressions loving and wise.

The second poem, or suite of poems, was published in *Face to Face* (1990), and one reader was so intrigued he translated it into Welsh. It emerged from contemplation of the sea as an image of the vast depths of God's being.

Sea Pieces

The sound of the sea is an endless fascination
A kind of tense repose that disturbs imagination
Deep calling to deep in constant expectation.

The sound of the sea stimulates relaxation
A kind of restless space for active contemplation
Deep calling to deep in visible meditation.

The sound of the sea encourages celebration
A kind of eternal time in rhythmic concentration
Wave surmounting wave in harmonic intonation
Deep calling to deep in symphonic jubilation.

*

Around the cliffs and caves of seabird colonies
The screams of circling gulls
Echo and reverberate
  echo and reverberate
As the screams of children playing
  screams of fear and laughter
And the screams of families fraying
  screams of love and anger
Echo and reverberate
  echo and reverberate
Around the walls and ways of human settlements.

But after the storm and the wild overnight gales
Around the cliffs and caves of seabird colonies
There echoes and reverberates
  booms and resonates
The thunder of roaring breakers
Drowning the screams of gulls
As the thunder of warring conflict
Echoes and reverberates
  booms and resonates
Drowning the screams of children playing
Drowning the screams of families fraying
In a mightier roar of pain
That echoes and reverberates
  booms and resonates
Around the walls and ways of human settlements.

Around the cliffs and caves of seabird colonies
The infinite swell of the ocean
Absorbs and assimilates
  absorbs and assimilates
The screams of circling gulls
As ripples on the surface of the waves.

So the infinite swell of God's love
Absorbs and assimilates
   resolves and sublimates
The screams of joy and anger
   screams of pain and hunger
The screams of fear and need
   screams of fun and greed
Screams of excitement
   and screams of indictment
Screams of deprivation
   and screams of elation
The infinite swell of God's love
Absorbs and assimilates
   resolves and sublimates
As ripples on the waves of eternity
Around the walls and ways of human settlements.

*

The sea, a destructive creating power,
Carves out coastlines hour by hour;
Restless its constant activity.
The sea, a boundless rising swell,
Captures minds and casts its spell;
Deep its untold mystery.

Booming in chasms and hollow caves,
Throwing up its sparkling spray,
Catching the sunlight it glistens and gleams,
Reflecting the clouds it's gloomy and grey;
Ebbing and flowing its boiling tide,
Cascading foam on every rock,
Rolling breakers to the shore,
Sustaining life where seabirds flock,
Roaring a salty haze in the air,
Churning stones in its surge and suck,
Tossing seaweed in its surf,
The sea lifts floats that bob and duck.

Tempting kids to romp in its waves,
Daring people to swim and play,

Coaxing crews of men to fish
For abundant resources to pay their way,
Carrying boats and ships to ply
Their dirty trade from dock to dock,
In hopes of making more and more
To stack behind a security lock,
Without obligation to play it fair,
Only to gamble with chance and luck,
The sea exacts a price for its job
Of mopping up countless gallons of muck.

The sea, an immense and playful giant,
To moon and wind responsive, pliant,
Yet with profound integrity,
Is like that infinite ocean of grace,
That surging tide which must give place
To be exploited and be free,
That awful creative love unknown,
Holy, hidden only shown
In ripples of still small secrecy,
That passionless deep beyond all sense,
That rages with passion deep and intense –
Mercy in wrath's serenity.

*

To be by the sea is an endless fascination
A kind of restless peace that imparts exhilaration
Deep resounding to deep with increasing exultation.

To be by the sea excites contemplation
A kind of awful joy and ecstatic sublimation
Deep resounding to deep with profound inner prostration.

To be by the sea is to join in veneration
A kind of endless praise for the wonder of creation
Wave reflecting wave in silent celebration
Deep responding to deep in endless circulation.

That poem tried to capture the idea that, for God, creation is a kind of abandonment, that God's absence is the reality within which we live, that God loves and lets go, so as to allow beings other than God to be themselves; and yet God is the one in whom we live and move and have our being, a presence holding the whole world in his hands, a creator who never ceases engaging in a hidden process of purifying our pollution. For neither Simone Weil nor the Bible would approve of the idea of deism – that God set off the whole process and then left it to its own devices. Rather God is continually engaged, though not as an omnipotent and triumphant fixer, but through a hands-off, hidden, elusive, loving and redeeming presence.

A classic story is found in Genesis 45. The backstory is typically human: jealousy led Joseph's brothers to plot against him, selling him off to traders going down to Egypt. But now Joseph is Pharaoh's powerful administrator, and famine has driven his brothers to Egypt to seek grain. Without having any idea who he is, they are completely dependent on Joseph's response. Furthermore, so as to get them in his power, Joseph has contrived to make them look like thieves. But now comes the moment when Joseph is overcome with emotion and his mask falls: 'I am Joseph,' he says. 'Is my father still living?' The brothers are so terrified they cannot answer. He calls them close and says, 'I am your brother, Joseph, the one you sold into Egypt! And now, do not be distressed and angry with yourselves for selling me here, because it was to save lives that God sent me ahead of you ... So then it was not you who sent me here, but God.' Somehow this extraordinary statement provides a key to the whole narrative of the Bible. This God is one who's let go, allowing the brothers to be free to sin – not a coercing, preventing, intervening God. Yet providentially somehow this same God has enabled a good outcome from that sinful act. To descry God in the mess of human history takes prophetic discernment – the traces are never obvious or discrete from human acts. Yet those with eyes to see may see, rejoice and give thanks.

As for Simone Weil, let me quote her again:

> God's creative love which maintains us in existence is not merely a super-abundance of generosity, it is also renunciation and sacrifice ... His love maintains in existence, in a free and autonomous existence, beings other than himself ... It is by an inconceivable love that he comes down so far as to reach them ... The Creation is a kind of passion. My very existence is like a laceration of God, a laceration which is love.[7]

If God has to let 'nothingness' be so that something other than God might come into being, then God's creativity is hardly comparable to human creativity: 'My thoughts are not your thoughts, nor are your ways my ways, says the LORD' (Isa. 55.8). We need a critique of that 'craftsman' analogy, indeed of all accounts of God's creativity drawn from straightforward parallels with human ways of doing things, including Intelligent Design. '*God is not an alternative to science as an explanation* . . . [God] is the ground of all explanation.'[8] Containing, yet uncontained, the infinite God emptied the divine self in a creative act of self-constriction – something like that has to be affirmed as the beginning of the finite, time-bound universe, astonishingly brought into being out of nothing. For God, creation meant loving and letting go.

How easy it is to begin prayers with the traditional phrase, 'Almighty God . . .'! For a period I self-consciously paused each time and began again – 'Loving God, Lord of compassion . . .' The very phrase 'Lord of compassion' contains the paradox of Christian theology. It's the relinquishing of Lordship, the challenge to our earthly notions of power, the *kenosis* or self-emptying of God which should provide the starting point of Christian thinking. Jesus washed his disciples' feet and asked his followers to take up the cross as he did. The limitless divine submitted to limitation, accepted vulnerability, lost control by being handed over to those who sought to destroy him.[9] Life itself died! In Christian theology this is more than rhetoric, it's revelation – revelation of God's self-limiting love, revelation of our calling: not to think of ourselves more highly than we ought to think, but to have the same mind that was in Christ Jesus,

> who, though he was in the form of God,
>> did not regard equality with God
>> as something to be exploited,
> but emptied himself,
>> taking the form of a slave,
>> being born in human likeness.
> And being found in human form,
>> he humbled himself
>> and became obedient to the point of death –
>> even death on a cross.   (Phil. 2.6–8)

A critique of power and dominance lies at the very heart of the gospel. Self-limitation so as to ensure that others are preferred, respected and waited on is the upside-down world of the New Testament. Every true pastor has surely had the experience of being humbled by the

Christ-like grace of someone living a small life of extreme vulnerability, suffering or pain – humbled but also strengthened and encouraged. Our God is a God of small things.

Limitation and bodiliness

In his study of parables, John Dominic Crossan[10] tells a story about a person sitting in a waiting room who, to pass the time, places a plastic cup a certain distance away, and tries to throw coins into it. Three hours later when the train arrives, he's thrown the coin over a hundred times, and landed it in the cup exactly once. If he'd got the coin in every time, there'd have been no point in the game. The game depends on limitation, and 'you tolerate a higher, even a total, failure rate more readily than you will tolerate a total or even high success rate'.

I was thinking about these things when Peter Humble told a re-inforcing story. A fisherman died. On regaining consciousness he found himself beside an ideal mountain stream in Scotland, thinking what a wonderful place, and if only he had his rod and line. Someone came and said if he wanted to fish, there was tackle available, and he could choose what he liked; the only condition was that once he'd made up his mind about equipment and location, he had to stick with it. So he chose the best tackle and the best place at the stream side. He cast, and immediately landed a fish – wonderful! He cast again, and immediately landed another perfect trout. When this happened a third time, he said, 'I'll go a bit further upstream.' But he was reminded of the conditions. He blurted out, 'Can't you do what you like in heaven?' The punchline was, 'Who said you were in heaven, sir?' But my point is this: perfection was too much for him!

These two stories suggest that when it comes down to it we need our 'handicaps' more than we imagine. So maybe God's creative purpose is not the attainment of utopia, individual fulfilment or indeed static perfection, which soon palls. Gregory of Nyssa, the fourth-century bishop mentioned earlier, has interesting things to say about per-fection. In the intellectual climate of his day, mutability (that is, our susceptibility to change) was seen as a major problem connected with physicality, with our bodily existence, something from which humanity needed salvation. The great insight Gregory contributed was that, on the contrary, mutability was both the consequence of our creation, of changing from being nothing to being something, and the condition of advance towards Godlikeness. To put it in our terms, limitation is required if humanity is to have potential, to be stretched towards ever higher goals. Gregory spoke of *epektasis* – a word borrowed from Paul (Phil. 3.13) meaning 'straining forward to what lies ahead'.

One of the earliest attempts to construct a system of Christian theology (that of Origen) began with the notion of a perfect heaven in which all created beings were enjoying contemplation of God. But that perfect state had clearly come to an end. How? Why? The solution was that these heavenly beings got literally 'fed up', overfull like a child tired of chocolate when it's had enough, satiated and bored with gazing on the divine. They needed a distraction, a sensation. Hence the fall from perfection and the creation of the material world as a school to train people for a return to heaven. Return to that heaven, however, would clearly be unstable. Gregory saw that static perfection was as uninviting as the fisherman's paradise. For Gregory, the spiritual journey was infinite, for no finite being can ever reach the end of the riches of the knowledge of the infinite God. Perfection has to be seen in dynamic as well as corporate terms, and human limitation is essential to the process.

Furthermore, like other early Christian writers, Gregory knew that we were created as bodily beings, that humans are composed of physical and spiritual elements, that we are (as I argued in Chapter 2) psychosomatic wholes. So for him, despite an intellectual climate favouring immortality of the soul, the resurrection meant the restoration of that wholeness, the raising up of the body, its transformation through refinement and purification, to be a 'spiritual body' fit for the new creation (compare 1 Cor. 15). No matter what the difficulties and objections, the early Christians insisted on this. That's why it's in the creed, and it makes a fundamental difference to the way bodies are viewed and treated – not as machines to be fixed by medical engineering but as sacrament, not as object but as sacred 'icon', integral to our encounter with the other person, no matter how wounded or sick. This has more than once been noticed as characteristic of the way L'Arche responds to the distorted and impaired bodies of the core members of the communities.

Bodily existence means being limited and vulnerable, and the whole point for the early Christians was to rise above this, to treat life as a kind of schooling, a testing. The culture of the time accepted that suffering and change were part and parcel of life and the Bible set this for them in the bigger perspective of being God's creatures, account-able to the Creator, while offering reasons for hope and confidence, for living life triumphantly, despite vulnerability and fragility. As Crossan puts it, 'Which do we prefer, comfort or courage? It may be necessary to make a choice.'

Brokenness and beauty

Jean Vanier speaks often of brokenness – of all his books one of the most beautiful is *The Broken Body*, written out of the depths of his experience in L'Arche and pondering the gospel story. Constantly he associates the fragility and brokenness of people with severe learning disabilities with the vulnerability and brokenness of Jesus Christ:

> There is a part of us that says
>> that brokenness is evil and should not exist . . .
> we want to live in a perfectly beautiful world,
>> a perfectly beautiful community,
>> a perfectly beautiful church . . .
> we are not allowed to be weak and broken,
>> fragile and vulnerable . . .
> . . . we are led to deny
> our own brokenness
>> and to despise the brokenness of others.

But then what about 'the broken body of Christ, limp, dirty, his face lined with agony, no beauty, no comeliness, a man of sorrows'? What about the disciples 'for whom everything is broken – the body of Jesus, their dreams, their hearts, their power, the body of their unity – all is broken, and all this brokenness seems only to recall their own inner decay and despair'? But 'it was through his littleness and pain, his brokenness and death, that Jesus saved them':

> By his broken body we, the body of humanity, are made whole.

> Our brokenness is the wound through which the power of God can penetrate our being and transfigure us in him.

So Jean explores how it is that 'the broken person reveals to you your own hurt – the one you came to heal becomes your healer'. One of the most profound challenges of L'Arche comes from the recognition that the way of Jesus is not patronizing do-good-ing, but a deep discovery of mutuality:

the recognition of our brokenness and of our wounds takes us off our pedestal and we discover the gift of these truths: we are no different from those we try to serve; we too are broken and wounded like them; we are a wounded people; but we can love each other, forgive each other and celebrate together our oneness.

You see, brokenness lies at the heart of Christian spirituality:

The sacrifice acceptable to God is a broken spirit;
a broken and a contrite heart, O God, you will not despise.

(Ps. 51.17)

All who exalt themselves will be humbled, and vice versa, says Jesus, summing up the parable of the proud over-religious person thanking God that he's so good compared with the miserable sinner beside him who can do nothing for himself but throw himself on God's mercy. 'There but for the grace of God go I,' said Charles Wesley as the condemned man went to the gallows. 'Where is your anguish?' asked Jean Vanier of a seminar of biblical scholars, challenging them to accept that you can only hear Scripture properly when your heart is broken.

So let me share my own 'heartbroken' interpretation of 2 Corinthians 4.7–11, as I did at the L'Arche IGA.

When God created, according to the story in Genesis 1, God said, 'Let there be light' and there was light. Later he put lamps in the sky, the bigger one to reign over the day, and the smaller one to reign over the night – we call them the sun and the moon. Lamps in the ancient world were like this, I said, and showed them a tiny replica to get the idea: a simple pot made of fired clay, it would be filled with oil and a wick stuck through the spout and lit. In the biblical world, light to chase away darkness came in earthenware vessels, clay pots.

When God created in the story as told in Genesis 2, he took dust, dampened it into clay and shaped a human figure – archaeologists have found little earthenware figurines all over the Middle East, and the storyteller probably had them in mind. Here I showed them a human figure from Guatemala made in baked clay – different kind of shape, coming from a different culture, but the same kind of thing. In Genesis, God fashions the clay figure of a person – something like this – and breathes life into it – so the figure became a living being and God put the person into the garden of Eden to till the soil and look after it.

These two moments in the biblical creation stories provide clues to what St Paul meant when he wrote that we have this treasure in clay pots. Light and life constitute this treasure, and it's contained in the equivalent of common clay jars, our human bodies. What I now suggested is that our experience of knowing and loving people with learning disabilities also provides clues to Paul's meaning. Through meditating on this image in Paul's second letter to the Corinthians, I set out to share ways in which L'Arche contributes to theology – to thinking about God and understanding the Scriptures.

I then showed them pots made in the workshops at L'Arche, Trosly-Breuil, explaining that pots people used in the biblical world would be all kinds of different shapes and sizes, and they were used for all kinds of different things. Their main use was storage. In John's Gospel at the wedding at Cana, six enormous pots full of water are part of the story – Jesus turns the water into wine and they ended up with gallons and gallons . . . Pots were part of everyday life, used to store grain and oil and other basic commodities.

But they were also used to hide precious things – money, jewels, treasure (at this point I put some chocolate money and various trinkets into the pot); and sometimes for another kind of treasure – books (again this was demonstrated). In the ancient world books were expensive luxury items and reading and writing was a professional skill, not something everyone was expected to do. One of the famous discoveries of ancient religious books was in Egypt in the 1940s at Nag Hammadi: peasants were digging for fertilizer and found pottery jars full of books.

So, it was usual for people to store things they cared about in common clay pots. Of course, when Paul says that we have this treasure in clay pots, he's probably implying a contrast with expensive metal containers, such as gold and silver vessels. That just reinforces the ordinariness at the heart of the metaphor or parable he's using. Treasure is secreted in ordinariness – it's hidden away for safe keeping, but present in ordinariness, not far away at the proverbial end of the rainbow and so an unattainable dream, nor the object of a long quest, as legend would have it. No – we have this treasure, present, in ordinary clay pots.

The treasure is light and life. The ordinary clay pots are our bodies. The clay vessel or figurine (held up again) was fashioned by God out of the dust and the life, or soul, was breathed into it. It's God's life which is contained in the clay pot. Treasure secreted in ordinariness implies that God's image is found in ordinary human being.

So next we worked through the passage of Scripture which contains this picture: 2 Corinthians 4, beginning with verse 5. In this letter Paul is discussing his own vocation and our extract begins with him pointing away from himself to Christ, and to his commitment to the Christians in Corinth.

> For we do not proclaim ourselves; we proclaim Jesus Christ as Lord and ourselves as your slaves for Jesus' sake. (verse 5)

He goes on:

> For it is the God who said, 'Let light shine out of darkness', who has shone in our hearts to give the light of the knowledge of the glory of God in the face of Jesus Christ. (verse 6)

You see, Paul refers back to creation, as we did at the start. So when he next says 'we have this treasure in clay jars', we know the treasure he's talking about is the life and light given in creation. First he clarifies the point that in the face of Jesus we see the glory of the Creator God, who not only breathed life into human beings but through Jesus has shone light into people's hearts.

Probably this light also implies wisdom. Wherever the word 'treasure' appears in the Bible that Paul knew, it means wisdom, and in Colossians, another Pauline epistle, there's a reference in 2.3 to Christ in whom are hidden 'all the treasures of wisdom and knowledge'. Here the light in Jesus' face is the knowledge of God's glory.

So the treasure is light and life and wisdom. And it's hidden in clay, in ordinariness, in our vulnerable and fragile bodies. For Paul goes on:

> We have this treasure in clay jars, so that it may be made clear that this extraordinary power belongs to God and does not come from us. (verse 7)

You see, unlike containers made of precious metals, clay pots are expendable. They are cheap so can easily be replaced, and they need to be, because they are easily shattered (here a broken pot was displayed). Once broken, pots are not repairable. Mostly that's true of our mortal bodies.

In the modern Western world, people have generally forgotten the limitations and vulnerability of human life. The press reacts with shock-horror when there are accidents and people die or are seriously damaged. So much has been done, by the skills and success of medical science, to ensure that our ills are cured, our brokenness repaired and the expectation of life is ever prolonged, that most people somehow believe that everything should be perfect. Suffering and death, disfigurement and vulnerability are not comfortable things for the majority of people in the modern, Western world. Our culture lives on success-values and can't take failure. The cult of sport has exposed perfect bodies and encouraged their development through training and physical discipline – aiming to be gold and silver vessels rather than clay pots, we might say. Likewise women are seduced into emulating the exposed perfect bodies of those ideal models whose images are all around us in the media.

And this is where L'Arche comes in. Because we've perceived beauty in damaged bodies, treasure in vulnerable and fragile persons. I spoke of how I shared the L'Arche experience every night, feeding my severely disabled son and preparing his twisted and impaired body for bed. In the everydayness of attending to bodily functions, eating and defecating, washing and dressing, touching and caressing, the sanctity of bodies is acknowledged, and the presence of treasure within brokenness.

You see, when a clay pot is broken, it exposes the treasure! (Here a pot was turned round to reveal its side broken and a candle inside.)

Paul used this picture to reinforce the contrast between God's power and human weakness: let's reread it with the next few verses.

> We have this treasure in clay jars, so that it may be made clear that this extraordinary power belongs to God and does not come from us. We are afflicted in every way, but not crushed; perplexed, but not driven to despair; persecuted, but not forsaken; struck down, but not destroyed; always carrying in the body the death of Jesus, so that the life of Jesus may also be made visible in our bodies.   (2 Cor. 4.7–10)

Paul wants us to realize the paradox – the broken body of the crucified Christ is where light and life and beauty are to be found. So it's the broken, vulnerable, clay pots of our bodies which paradoxically bear testimony to God's power: God's glory, light, life and wisdom hidden in the ordinariness of fragile clay jars.

There's a long-standing tradition in Catholic piety of discerning the image of God not in the rich and powerful but rather in the poor.

This has motivated charitable works, and has been seen as fulfilling most directly the demands of the gospel. These days, I suggested, liberation theology claims that tradition, taking the option for the poor; but it also offers a critique, that charity can be patronizing, it can trap the poor in their poverty. When liberation theologians read their Bibles they see God on the side of the poor, and so they engage in activities which will empower the poor. They hold out hopes of changing the world, ending poverty, fulfilling the Magnificat, by bringing down the powerful and lifting up the lowly, filling the hungry with good things and sending the rich empty away. Of course in theory poverty could be eliminated if there was fair sharing. Liberation theologies are theologies of hope for the oppressed and marginalized.

In important ways, L'Arche shares that tradition. People with learning disabilities are particularly poor in terms of life's gifts and talents, as well as in social exclusion, economic deprivation and, most serious of all, human love and relationship. Like liberation theologies, L'Arche knows that charity is patronizing, and instead seeks mutual liberation. But in important ways L'Arche challenges liberation theologies. For the poverty of people with learning disabilities is simply not removable, at least not by human agency. People with learning disabilities are born that way, or become that way through brain damage which is incurable. L'Arche reminds us of the limits of human capacity to put things right. It obliges us to confront the vulnerability of human creatureliness and the false ideology of trying to turn this life into the perfect paradise everybody tends to dream of.

How is God on the side of these 'poor' people? Hope lies not in the removal of their condition, but in another dimension. Those who accompany persons in L'Arche discover that through our difference from one another is revealed something deeply significant about our common humanity. What develops is a theology of presence, in communion and community, a kind of contemplative waiting on God with one another, which is far removed from political activism or patronizing charity, and which accepts weakness, vulnerability and indeed death. There is a mutuality in which grace is imparted to each, and each gives and receives. We accord dignity to one another through our mutual respect. And we are all vulnerable and in need of salvation.

We find, like Paul, that God is present in the midst of this weak and creaturely existence, and that our calling is to reveal God's power in weakness. Hope lies not in a political vision of utopia and righting wrongs here and now but rather in the fruits of the spirit – love, joy, peace, patience, kindness, goodness, faithfulness, gentleness and self-control (Gal. 5.22). All of this means that, through the vocation of L'Arche, dimensions of the Gospel come alive in new ways, and so does our reading of Scripture.

We have this treasure in clay pots. Our clay pots are easily shattered, but that brokenness reveals the treasure within – the light and life and wisdom of God which we receive through Christ. So we are always *carrying in the body the death of Jesus, so that the life of Jesus may also be made visible in our bodies.* God's love and power is recognized through our mutual need and dependence. In the ordinary everyday business of living together, the divine image is discerned, secreted in the ordinariness of clay pots that are breakable, but in their brokenness expose the treasure within.

After speaking of the struggles and afflictions accompanying his vocation, Paul reaches a climax, one that we can affirm too in our experience of being called to live with people who have learning disabilities:

> Yes, everything is for your sake, so that grace, as it extends to more and more people, may increase thanksgiving, to the glory of God.
>
> (2 Cor. 4.15)

5

The cross and redemption

The Tree of Life

He looked up at the trees
  and I followed his gaze
  to behold
  a moving kaleidoscope
    of light and shade
    tossed in the breeze.

He looked up at the trees
  and I followed his gaze
  to behold
    a knotted rope dangling
    and nails and thorns
    plaited and keys.

He looked up at the trees
  and I followed his gaze
  to behold
    a still winter skeleton
    an outline sharp
    etched on the skies.

He looked up at the trees
  and I followed his gaze
  to behold
    a sticky bud bursting
    with life, and death
    touched with surprise.

Arthur loves trees. One day he smiled up at the trees in the garden, and I saw reality in all its dimensions, its beauty and its ambiguity, its tragedy and transcendence. That poem was the result, picking up the old tradition of calling the cross the tree of life. The meaning of Christ's crucifixion is the other major theological area where Arthur has given me privileged access to the deepest truths of Christianity. This chapter will explore questions about tragedy, judgement and redemption, key concepts where my theological reflections have been enhanced by the context provided by Arthur and others like him.

As indicated earlier, my journey through the wilderness first led me to the cross as the place to meet God. I discovered how God in Jesus entered into all the 'gone-wrongness' of the world and transformed it into glory: that was the insight which began the process of renewing my battered faith. The cross became for me the proper Christian answer to the problem of suffering. But what do we mean by 'gone-wrongness'? The previous chapter might be read as an attempt to suggest that all's right with the world after all. That's not, however, the way things feel. Some 'evils' are clearly put into proper perspective as 'natural': things like the pain which is a warning sign when you touch a hot plate, the bite of a mosquito and the malaria parasite it carries, volcanic eruptions, destructive storms and floods, the mutation or accident which results in infant malformation, and indeed death itself. From the point of view of the created earth as a whole, even the four horses of the Apocalypse – war, famine, plague and wild beasts (Rev. 6) – can be regarded as good: mechanisms to keep the human population under control and the ecology of the planet in balance, mechanisms our cleverness has upset, with potentially dire consequences. But that observation just reinforces the point that from our point of view the world seems set up for excessive suffering – suffering which is further compounded by what the Christian tradition calls sin. A colleague of Jewish descent once said to me, 'If I were God I wouldn't let my children do to each other the things we do.' In the wake of the Holocaust, what reply could one offer? Our sense of 'gone-wrongness' encompasses suffering and the sin which exacerbates it. Life can appear to be altogether tragic. The story of the cross is itself a tragedy – the torture and elimination of an innocent. So how is it redemptive?

Tragedy as life-giving

Tragedy is a word which frequently appears in everyday speech in our society, capturing general horror at the awful things treated as newsworthy. Though himself so limited as to be unaware of it, Arthur's life many would regard as tragic, a life doomed from the start to helplessness, uselessness, meaninglessness. Some living with impairment would resist the idea that their situation involves either suffering or tragedy – they're simply who they are and should be respected as such. However, it's hard for most people not to react to shocking loss of function as anything other than tragic. Admiration for the courage and determination of those who overcome their impairments and, despite everything, achieve great things, say in the Paralympics, just compounds the sense of the tragic in more extreme cases like Arthur's. Tragedy, then, is normally viewed in entirely negative terms, but what I want to suggest is that, contrary to expectation, it's through tragedy that we discover what is most deeply life-giving, and that the clue is provided by the cross, along with lives like Arthur's.

Studying literature in my younger years, long before becoming a theologian, I felt that it was in tragedy that one plumbed the depths of what it means to be human. Decades later I would begin to discern that tragedy might illuminate the meaning of the cross more profoundly than the atonement theories offered by historical theology. For, like sacrifice, tragic drama probably originated as a ritual enabling people to deal with the 'gone-wrong' elements in human existence, together with the horrific realities of human behaviour, both collective and individual. What I'll try to explain is how putting doom and death into a ritual context could turn it into a means of purification and atonement, thus transforming it into something life-giving.

We live a story-shaped existence and have a story-shaped identity. We understand the world – indeed, create our own story – through entering the stories we're told as children, the narratives we read, the drama we watch on film or TV. Roughly speaking, stories reflect two fundamental views of life, the 'tragic' and the 'comic', the latter being marked by resolution – the happy ending. What constitutes the essence of tragedy is a much discussed topic, and it's not easy to come up with any generally applicable formula. But we can trace key elements in an example.

T. S. Eliot's *Murder in the Cathedral* is a modern drama written from within a Christian world-view, yet it's modelled on the classical form of ancient Greek tragedy. The play opens with the Chorus full of foreboding and articulating one notion common to much tragic literature – that life is beyond one's control:

Destiny waits in the hand of God, not in the hand of statesmen
Who do, some well, some ill, planning and guessing,
Having their aims which turn in their hands in the pattern of time.

The women of the Chorus are 'the poor', for whom 'there is no action,
But only to wait and to witness'; they represent 'the common man',
the 'human kind' which 'cannot bear very much reality', immersed
in the trivialities of the domestic process of keeping alive, 'living
and partly living'. They want to be left in peace. But by the end of
the play they're praying for forgiveness – for they too are exposed as
implicated. If we say that we have no sin, there is no health in us.

The Knights who perpetrate the deed are full of self-justification,
excuses, whitewashes, making out that there were no alternatives,
as in all arguments for a just war, all acts of oppression, even little
dishonesties ... In matter-of-fact prose, which contrasts with the
poetry of the rest of the play, they reveal their blindness to their own
responsibility. An exposure, a judgement, is going on.

But then there's the tragic hero, Thomas. Fully conscious of the
possibilities, he faces up to the temptations of his position. Last but
not least is the possibility that acceptance of vocation may itself be
corrupt and self-seeking – to be the glorious martyr! How marvellous!
Until purged of that tainted pride, Thomas cannot be the true
martyr, whatever happens. What you are is more important than
what you do:

> The last temptation is the greatest treason:
> To do the right deed for the wrong reason ...
> Sin grows with doing good ...

The terrible truth emerges that our worst faults may be the inescapable
obverse of our greatest virtues – more exposure of the ambiguities
of human action and moral choice.

In this presentation of Thomas Becket, Eliot demonstrates how
truth is found not in facts but rather in the mysterious depths which
have to be explored through rituals acknowledging pollution and shame,
and opening up the possibility of purgation. Studies of tragedy[11] show
how the themes of fate and flaw recur. The protagonist is caught
up in things beyond his or her control, and/or has faults of character
which lead to deeds which have a strange inevitability, yet are his/her
responsibility. So tragedy's subject matter is the vulnerability of human
greatness, the contingencies and dilemmas of human existence, the

interplay of luck and choice, and the paradox that in practice we hold people responsible for what they do, even when the cards are stacked against them. Tragedy sensitively explores impossible choices, where deeply held moral principles are in conflict, and there's no right decision – whatever choice is made, there will be guilt. While 'comedy gives voice to a fundamental trust in life', 'the tragic vision isolates the hero over against an arbitrary and capricious world, a world in which ... the problem of evil is irreducible and unresolvable into some larger, harmonious whole'. Yet the very act of presenting it invests the unintelligible with some kind of meaning; and tragedy becomes a creative and therefore inherently redemptive engagement with the mystery of the ambiguities and darkness of human existence. The drama or narrative gives order to the hidden depths we prefer to keep veiled, thus becoming a performative act of resolution and reconciliation.

In classical Athens, tragedy arose in a ritual context. The action presented the story in song and dance as part of a religious festival, and it was a liturgy performed before, and on behalf of, the whole community. Aristotle wrote that tragedy 'through the arousal of pity and fear effected the *katharsis* of such emotions'. There's been a tendency to understand this in terms of a great 'emotional steam-bath', as the great director Peter Brook once put it. But if *katharsis* is taken seriously in its religious context, it has a rather different implication. For *katharsis* means purification.

In her book *Purity and Danger* the anthropologist Mary Douglas explains how primitive peoples took things that were taboo, like blood and death, and by putting these fearful things into a ritual context, sacralized them, transforming them from being life-denying to life-affirming: 'The special kind of treatment which some religions accord to anomalies and abominations to make them powerful for good is like turning weeds and lawn cuttings into compost.' That's what sacrifice was all about: it took the taboo substance blood and turned it into a means of purification. What was involved was a shift in perspective as the taboo subject was handled and faced and put into another context. 'The ceremony of animal sacrifice ... expressed the awe and fear felt by this human community towards its own murderous possibilities.' By ritually killing an animal and surrounding this killing 'with a ceremony indicative of the killers' innocence and their respect for life', the sacrificers both acknowledged and distanced themselves from their potential for violence. Tragedy most probably originated from sacrifice, then, and works in the same way: it makes it possible for human beings to avoid escapism, to confront things they dare not face. Normally we cannot stand too much reality, but here we can. In great tragic drama we are enabled to face up to those things about the human condition we would rather forget or deny. So Peter Brook suggests that there is 'Holy Theatre': 'We are all aware that most of life escapes our senses. We know that the world of appearance is a crust – under the crust is the boiling matter we see if we peer into a volcano.'

In theatre, the 'invisible becomes visible'; we find liberation from our ordinary everyday selves. This is what makes 'the theatre a holy place in which a greater reality could be found', often in the paradox of a loss which is also gain. Great tragedy probes for the meaning behind it all. It exposes the truth about the human condition so that it may be faced and ritually dealt with. Is this not what we saw embodied in Eliot's play?

Now some would claim that there can be no genuinely tragic vision within Christianity. The resurrection provides the happy ending that simply turns the Christian story into comedy. But inherent in the New Testament, certainly in the Passion narratives and even in the resurrection stories, is a deeply tragic element. For in tragedy, as Nietzsche put it, 'one stares at the inexplicable'. Mark's Gospel, though its language is the crude rough Greek of a Palestinian, is written with unconscious literary art. All participants are exposed as implicated in the deed, as in Eliot's tragedy; the central figure of the drama foresees the destiny he has to face, struggles with it in Gethsemane, and then is progressively isolated, misunderstood, betrayed by a friend, denied by his right-hand man, despised, rejected, finally forsaken even by the God whose will he strove to perform. As the tragedies of ancient Greece found meaning in the interplay of necessity and choice, so Mark makes it clear that this is the playing out of the destiny long foreshadowed – in ancient prophecies, in terrible tales like the sacrifice of Isaac – yet freely chosen. 'Increasingly one sees that the reality of Christ's humanity resides precisely in the fact that as he lived he was confronted with real choices, fraught, in consequence of the way in which he chose, with disaster as well as achievement in their train.' The victory 'remains mysteriously and inescapably tragic'.[12]

The Epistle to the Hebrews, though reflecting on the event rather than narrating it, draws out other features classic in tragedy: the paradox of one innocent yet guilty, as the sacrificial victim is without blemish yet ritually bears the sin of the people; the learning through suffering explored in Greek tragedy; the greatness, yet vulnerability, of one who struggles with the contingencies of the human condition, sharing in human flesh and blood, praying with loud cries and tears, yet able to sanctify those who share his human nature.

The cross, then, functions like tragedy. The drama exposes the reality of human sin, the insoluble conflicts which so often lead to the suffering of the innocent, the banishment and destruction of what is good, the mobilization of the political and religious structures to eliminate change or challenge. Christ is thrust outside the camp, banished like the scapegoat, destroyed so that purity could be maintained. All humanity is involved in the shame of it. Yet the story of the cross is redemptive. For the things we fear, the taboos of blood and death, the curse of the most cruel and despicable punishment devised by humanity, these are sacralized – put in a positive context in which they can be faced and dealt with. The drama effects an exposure of the truth. It becomes a universal narrative, a story told by an inspired poet, not a mere chronicler or historian. As Aristotle put it, 'poetry is both more philosophical and more serious than history, since poetry speaks of universals, history of particulars'. The terrible truth of human complicity in evil, of goodness snuffed out, of God's abandonment, is exposed and faced, faced as in a ritual context: the thing that is taboo is turned into something holy, the sin we cannot bear to face is redeemed, the pollution we usually fail to observe is revealed, and *katharsis*, in the sense of purification or atonement, is effected.

So does the resurrection undermine the force of the Passion? Of course, the resurrection may be presented as a dramatic reversal, as a 'comic' happy ending appended to the Passion. But it is not a simple reversal, a restoration that puts things back as if nothing had happened. No Christian believer would simply want to speak of resuscitation; every Christian believer would want to affirm transfiguration, metamorphosis of some kind. And it's this mystery that the Gospel narratives seek to convey. The resurrection stories are not tales of joyful recognition and the restoration of normality. The marks of the nails remain and are somehow trans-valued. Fear is mentioned far more than we generally notice. Mary is cruelly brushed off as she tries to make contact with the Jesus she knew: 'Do not cling to me, for I have not yet ascended to the Father.' His presence with her and with the disciples is fraught with ambiguity, with an open and terrifying future, insecurity. So there is a hiddenness and awfulness which belies any sense of triumph. Pilate and the powers of oppression remain untouched, and whatever resolution there is is like the mystery of tragic drama. Those who witness this passionate action are enabled to gaze on the reality of death and the reality of God – the taboo and terrifying reality of which humanity cannot bear too much.

It's John's Gospel that most effectively holds together cross and resurrection, as the Passion becomes the hour of glory, the pain, suffering, sin, guilt, destiny, darkness, vulnerability to death and the powers of evil; indeed, the frighteningly inexplicable becomes even more inexplicably the theophany, the blinding dazzling light of exposure, judgement, revelation. It is in tragedy rather than comedy that one expects to confront the *mysterium tremendum et fascinans* – the mystery that's both fearful and fascinating – the Holy One, and to be moved with pity and terror, with awe and fear of the Lord. So the drama of Christ's death and resurrection as a whole first presents us with the realities of pain and loss, sin and judgement, suffering and death – all the intertwined 'gone-wrongness' of the human condition. Then, as I discovered through contemplating the healing of the blind man in John 9 (see Chapter 2), it shows us God taking responsibility for it all, bearing it all, not wafting it all away with a magic wand, but profoundly transforming it from within. The tragedy of the cross holds the promise that the most terrible things we face, and even tragedies like Arthur's, may find transformation *within* their reality, not by magic reversal – for the cross of Christ is about God's love staying with us in the midst of it all. This was the hour of glory I witnessed on Good Friday in Lourdes (see Chapter 3).

Sin, suffering and judgement

As tragedy explores fate and flaw, necessity and choice, destiny and death, so the Bible ponders the deep connections between sin, suffering and judgement. Both Scripture and tragic literature, such as *Murder in the Cathedral*, alert us to the fact that we're all implicated in the way things have gone wrong. In John's Gospel the cross is not only the hour of glory, but also the judgement of the world. Judgement became an important aspect of my reflections in the first versions of *Face to Face*. For one of the intriguing aspects of John's Gospel is the way in which judgement is inbuilt into the story. Jesus did not come to judge:

> God sent the Son into the world, not to condemn the world, but that the world might be saved through him. (John 3.17, RSV)

But judgement happens anyway:

> This is the judgement, that the light has come into the world and [human beings] loved darkness rather than light, because their deeds were evil. For every one who does evil hates the light, and does not come to the light, lest his deeds should be exposed.
> (John 3.19–20, RSV)

Judgement is exposure. When things go wrong we're shown up for what we are, by the way we react, the way we cope. So all mishap, all suffering, is a kind of judgement in that it is a crisis (the Greek word *krisis* means judgement) which discriminates in this way. Furthermore, you can't simply divide suffering from judgement. Suffering is quite often our fault – a road accident may be the outcome of a genuine accident like a tyre blown out, or it may be the result of diabolical driving or inadequate maintenance. Cancer or a heart attack may be a desperately sad chance – but increasingly research suggests that habits and lifestyle, diet, smoking, and so on, may well be contributors. We don't like the doctrine that suffering is the result of sin, because we're all too aware that there is much innocent suffering. But if we approve what Jesus said about the man born blind – that it was not his sin or the sin of his parents, which caused him to be born blind (John 9.3) – we should also note the story in which he offered the paralytic forgiveness before he healed him (Mark 2.5). There is a connection between suffering and judgement, between our mistakes, our faults, our habits, and our reaping the consequences of them. Even if we cannot accept this in the case of all individual suffering, plainly there is suffering because people *en masse* behave badly. We're all in it together.

Disability brings about a kind of judgement. I certainly don't mean it's punishment for sin. It's seldom anyone's fault. Some disabilities may be the consequence of careless or blameworthy acts, some may be the fault of a society that allows certain kinds of pollution; but many arise from sheer accidents or genetic mutations – they just happen. Yet disability does bring about judgement, a *krisis*, because it's a kind of test. It discriminates between those who rise to the occasion and those who fail to do so. It discriminates between the good marriage and the shaky marriage, the stable family and the unstable family. It shows up people, their relationships and their values, for what they are. Society is judged by the way it treats disabled people and our society is ambiguous. On the one hand, there's real concern and genuinely progressive thinking, on the other indifference and even disability hate crime – instances of exploitation or cruelty surface regularly in our newspapers, not to mention cases of abuse in care homes. Judgement occurs through exposure.

As I was writing this book, an article appeared in the *Guardian* newspaper by Ian Birrell (22 May 2013). It began like this:

> My daughter was ill at the weekend. Just a heavy cold; but when your child has profound and multiple learning disabilities, even a minor illness can send her life-threatening condition spiralling out of control, so we needed to get some antibiotics. As so often it was a dispiriting experience.

Not only did he go on to describe his own less than satisfactory experience with NHS staff, he also reported a distressing case of a young woman with disabilities who died after a series of blunders, and quoted her mother:

> When your child becomes ill and you need professional help from doctors, you and your child are looked at and you can see them thinking, 'Is there any point in trying to save this child's life?' You can see that they think, 'This child has an existence and not a life.'

Then he drew attention to a government-commissioned inquiry into one region, which found people with disabilities 37 per cent more likely to be killed by incompetence or inadequate care – that their lives end on average 16 years earlier than they should. The more serious the disabilities, the higher the risk. He noted that Mencap, while blaming poor communication with parents and carers as the main cause, concluded that the only explanation for so many preventable deaths is prejudice – doctors and nurses reflect views prevalent across society that people with profound disabilities are second-class citizens, their lives not worth saving. He went on to comment:

> There is a shameful failure to understand that every life is different, yet all have the same value. This is the fumbling bigotry – and that is the only word for it – that emerges when people tell a grieving parent their son or daughter is perhaps better off dead. This is the starker bigotry that explains the rise in hate crime, the reluctance of employers to hire people with disabilities, the resurgence of eugenics. It explains why disabled people live under a form of apartheid, for all the hot air around the Paralympics.

A previous *Guardian* article of his (16 October 2010) explored disturbing instances of disability hate crime, highlighting cases of violence, the bullying of persons with learning disabilities by callous youths, the abuse which drove a mother to murder her disabled daughter and commit suicide. But somehow the respectable lack of acceptance highlighted here is more disturbing, providing as it does the lower level and pervasive background to scandals in so-called care homes. I should say that with Arthur we've mostly had good experiences with people we've had to deal with in the NHS, and indeed the general public, though I can't say the same about dealing with administrators about his benefits – suspicion seems to be their default position. As indicated in *Face to Face*, experience of heartless and inefficient bureaucracies certainly makes me sorry for those less articulate and more disadvantaged than we happen to be. Society would rather not bear the cost of disability. People in general think that persons with disabilities, especially those most profoundly impaired, don't deserve to live, not least because they evidently make no contribution to society – indeed, they are a drain on it.

Yet, looking back I can see that my own questions implied a perspective not too dissimilar. Worrying about how I could go on believing in a good Creator implied that Arthur's life I regarded as not worthwhile. That perception was compounded by the periods of his inexplicable misery: why should he have to suffer on top of every-thing else? Why couldn't one just put him out of his misery, as one would a damaged bird or a horse with a broken leg? What was the point of it all? Do people like him have a significant role to play? The school doctor once said to me, 'Society needs handicap' (handicap being accepted usage at the time). How could that be true?

Redemptive relationships

'The Crooked Timber of Humanity' – that was the title of my lecture, a tape of which was sent to Jean Vanier, that began my association with L'Arche. It was mighty controversial. The posters went up, and naturally enough, the quotation I'd chosen as my title was misunderstood, appearing as it did in association with the subtitle – 'the challenge of the handicapped'. Just as I was about to prepare the lecture, I received a protest letter, which caused me profound upset – anger that anyone could think a parent would say what they thought I was saying, embarrassment at my own failure to anticipate how it might be read. In the event, however, it sharpened up the argument. It provided a raw example of exactly the issue I intended to address: namely, social acceptance of persons with profound disabilities.

So the lecture began with that protest letter and asked what was the source and intention of the title. The phrase came from the philosopher Immanuel Kant. The full sentence reads: 'Out of the crooked timber of humanity can nothing straight be made.' Clearly he meant, as I meant, the whole of humanity. But this statement unfortunately took on a life of its own in the minds of some who saw the phrase on posters abstracted from the full quotation. Why did the phrase signify something derogatory or insulting? Clearly because it was expected to. Why was that? Because of experience that there's something twisted in human response to those with disabilities. Many parents have some tale to tell of rejection or prejudice, ostracism or audible remarks that hurt – like the couple I once knew who couldn't bear to take their family on holiday because if they sat on the beach they could feel everyone staring. I reminded the audience of a public scandal a few years before. In Teignmouth in Devon, those who earned their living in the tourist trade, the hotel-keepers, the shopkeepers, the Chamber of Commerce, protested about the numbers of people with learning disabilities coming to the town on holiday or for day outings. There was a press uproar and clearly most people felt they should have known better. But the point I wanted to make – being honest if a little blunt – was this: it's hard to be natural about people with disabilities, because they don't fit. It's no good being sentimental about it.

People with disabilities trigger gut reactions in people. There was a time, I said, when I felt very aggressive about this, and rather

107

belligerently determined that we should live as normal a life as possible and other people would have to accept Arthur. But you cannot
force integration. Nor can you simply condemn those people who
cannot cope with their feelings. Even I had found it distressing to
go to functions at my own son's school – it just deepened the pain.
Instead of pretending things are otherwise, we need to consider why
this is the way things are and what might be done about it. Part
of the problem is fear – fear of the unknown. Acceptance can only
follow understanding. Our difficulties with accommodating people
with learning disabilities have the same roots as racism. It's because
people are like us but different that we find it so hard simply to be
natural. But there are also those indefinable fears that arise in people
when they see someone blind or in a wheelchair – that vague and
unadmitted fear that it might be me – because the disabled person
is too like us for comfort. Do we stare or do we look away? It's like
the horrified fascination that draws crowds to the scene of an accident.

The lecture then drew on Mary Douglas' book *Purity and Danger*
to help explain why as human beings we react the way we do.
Endeavouring to understand religious regulations like the distinction
between clean and unclean foods in the book of Leviticus, she pointed
out that every society has its 'purity' regulations. Purity implies the
removal of dirt. Dirt is relative – just 'matter out of place'. Food's not
dirty in itself, but it is dirty to leave cooking utensils in the bedroom
or food spattered on clothing. Dirt implies a 'set of ordered relations
and contravention of that order ... Where there is dirt there is system.
Dirt is the by-product of a systematic ordering and classification of
matter.' Our apprehension of the world involves the development of
a culture which organizes our perceptions, classifies and labels, and
as individuals, we are educated into the culture of the social group
to which we belong. 'Culture ... provides in advance some basic
categories, a positive pattern in which ideas and values are tightly
ordered.' My mother told me my first words were 'pretty' and 'dirty'.

The ordered system whereby the world is classified, known and
understood, however, is challenged by what Douglas calls 'anomalies'
and 'ambiguities' – things that do not fit predetermined categories.
Her argument is that the desire for purity proves to be 'hard and
dead', that 'purity is the enemy of change'. The crucial thing is how
a society copes with anomalies. It may exclude, or reinterpret within
the system. Or it may respond so as to generate something creative.

The things that do not fit, the marginal or liminal, may produce revulsion, shock or laughter, but also provoke novelty. There is power in the margins. Religious ritual, she suggests, is a way of dealing with taboo and terrible things so as to produce cleansing and new life. She suggests a parable (mentioned earlier): the gardener tidies, orders, or we might say 'purifies' the garden by taking out the weeds. If the weeds are burned or thrown away, that is that. But if the weeds are turned into compost, then the 'anomalies' become life-giving. So sacrifice turned the taboo substance blood into a life-giving and atoning reality.

Human societies do not naturally welcome difference. Our hunter-gatherer ancestors could not support anyone infirm or incapable, whether through age, injury or disability. They had to find ways of reinterpreting the birth of an 'anomaly', to deal with the challenge and shock. Mary Douglas gives an example from the Nuer tribe:

> when a monstrous birth occurs, the defining lines between humans and animals may be threatened. If a monstrous birth can be labelled an event of a peculiar kind the categories can be restored. So the Nuer treat monstrous births as baby hippopotamuses, accidentally born to humans, and with this labelling, the appropriate action is clear. They gently lay them in the river where they belong . . .

Societies in the grip of high modernity did something somewhat similar when they employed the medical model as a way of justifying the exclusion of people with disabilities into hospitals. The early twentieth-century fascination with genetic purity reinforced that and led to the Nazi policy of 'cleansing' society of people with defects, as well as those with the wrong ethnicity like Jews and gypsies.

But these natural attempts to achieve purity, as Mary Douglas suggests, prevent the creative from happening. It's when these tendencies are exposed, judged and transformed that profound breakthroughs can occur. L'Arche has discovered that 'they' have the power to evangelize 'us' – in other words, the people who are disadvantaged, disabled, poverty-stricken in more ways than one, have the capacity to 'convert' those of us who appear to have capabilities they lack. The Greek word usually translated 'repentance' actually means 'change of mind', and this 'conversion' requires a process of exposure or judgement so as to effect a fundamental change in attitudes. This can only come through transforming mutual relationships.

In the original lecture, given before I knew L'Arche first-hand, I suggested that the key lies in establishing reciprocal relationships with those who have disabilities. The most fundamental aspect of this is the recognition not that we do them good but that they do something for us. I confessed that what finally resolved my personal distress was the discovery that I had to give thanks for Arthur, that it was no longer a case of accepting him, but rejoicing in him and receiving from him. I quote:

> I come in bruised and battered from the trials and tribulations of the world, the pressures of University cuts and problem students, and awful committees and people needing me and making demands on me, and there is Arthur to be fed and changed, bathed and lifted, put to bed and got up, in an endless and sometimes wearisome routine – but that is not the whole story. Where I minister to others, Arthur ministers to me. He shows me what life is about, brings me down to basics, gives me peace, helps me to resolve the tensions, and it is with him that I find the fruits of the Spirit, love, joy, peace, patience, kindness, goodness, faithfulness, humility and self-control.

I then went on to describe how a couple of students had gone on holiday the previous year with Arthur and the Catholic Handicapped Children's Fellowship, how they went as helpers but returned euphoric, if exhausted – it had quite literally been a conversion experience in which they had come to a quite new appreciation of what life was all about. If we are to be truly human, I suggested, we need to over-come fears and embarrassment and relate to persons with disabilities. This would be the way of redemption from the crookedness explored earlier in the lecture. And what it means, I said, is that it's not so much those with disabilities who need community care, but society in general.

An amazing example of the redemptive presence of someone with learning disabilities turned up as I was putting this chapter together. I was reading *The Hunger Angel*, a book by the Nobel prize-winning novelist, Herta Müller, which tells the story of ethnic Germans from Romania and elsewhere in Eastern Europe who, at the end of the Second World War, were deported into labour camps to rebuild Russia by the victorious Soviet forces. In the form of a novel, it draws on actual reminiscences. One of the characters is Kati Sentry, a woman described as 'born feeble-minded', and completely unaware of where she was: 'Kati Sentry wasn't suited for any type of work. She didn't understand what a quota was, or a command, or a punishment. She disrupted the course of the shift . . .' So they found her a sentry job – hence her name. The persistent refrain of the book is the sheer hunger they all suffered, and how they exploited one another to get bread. But no one was allowed to take Kati Sentry's bread.

> In the camp we've learned to clear away the dead without shuddering. We undress them before they turn stiff, we need their clothes so we won't freeze to death. And we eat their saved bread. Their death is our gain. But Kati Sentry is alive, even if she doesn't know where she is. We realize this, so we treat her as something that belongs to all of us. We make up for what we do to one another by standing up for her. We're capable of many things, but as long as she is living among us, there's a limit to how far we actually go.

The camp inmates were redeemed by the presence of a person with learning disabilities.

The Bible, too, points to the possibility that the 'outsider' can prove redemptive. I learned this from Ian Cohen, an Anglican priest and father of a son with severe epilepsy, whose constant fits meant that he was gradually losing brain function and abilities as he grew up. Speaking at a conference in Birmingham, Ian pointed out that, like liberation theology, biblical studies concerned with a theology of disability tend to focus on the 'marginalized', 'the poor' or 'disadvantaged'. But these images are of people who can be integrated if circumstances are changed; with the right kind of social organization the economically poor need not be so. Looking for a biblical model for those whose condition cannot be changed, persons like our own disabled sons, Ian proposed the *gēr*, the Hebrew word for the 'sojourner' or 'resident alien', a 'protected or dependent foreigner'. Neither an Israelite nor a slave, the *gēr* was to be treated fairly and protected against injustice and violence. The reason for this was that the *gēr* reflected the true soul of the Israelite:

> You shall not wrong a *gēr* or be hard on him; you were *gērim* yourselves in Egypt. (Exod. 22.21)

> You shall not oppress the *gēr* for you know how it feels to be a *gēr*; you were *gērim* yourselves in Egypt. (Exod. 23.9)

Ian showed how Abraham is depicted as a *gēr*, Joseph and his brothers are *gērim* in Egypt, Moses lived as a *gēr* in Midianite territory, Elijah experienced the lot of a *gēr*. In Egypt and the Exodus the Israelites had communal experience of having nowhere to call their own, and in the Promised Land they recited, 'My father was a homeless Aramaean who went down to Egypt . . .' as they gave thanks for the first-fruits. So being a *gēr* was deep in the Israelite identity, and they were to love the *gēr*, God being no respecter of persons and loving the alien who lived among them. The prophets pick up the theme, especially Jeremiah, who points to rediscovery of the soul of the *gēr* as important. He experiences being an 'outsider' himself because of his terrible message, and even hints that God would be 'as a *gēr*' (Jer. 14.8).

The person who is different, the literal stranger, the 'other', is thus a sign of what Israel truly is, and the 'outsider' prophet is a sign of God's otherness, God's strangeness. There is a belonging which is also not a belonging. For Ian Cohen this illuminated the strange belonging yet not belonging of the 'alien' child in the family, the strange child who is different, though 'bone of my bone and flesh of my flesh'. He then turned to the New Testament, especially 1 Peter: here the Church is a new Israel, a nation of sojourners: 'Beloved, I urge you *as aliens and exiles* to abstain from the desires of the flesh . . .' (2.11–12). Christians may be ethnically related to their pagan neighbours, but they have become different – aliens and exiles, sojourners, resident aliens, *paroikoi* (to use the Greek term). Christians live as strangers and exiles on earth. And they do so because even the risen Christ is accused of being a *paroikos* in the story of the walk to Emmaus; and the Psalms which speak of being a *gēr* (Psalm 39, for example) have their parallels in the Passion narratives. Ian's deduction was that we should not care for those with disabilities because that does us good – that would be patronizing charity. Rather we care for them because they reveal to us who we really are – that is how 'the Other' matters. As *gērim* they show us that we too have the soul of the *gēr*. Through them we may enter into redemptive relationships.

Judgement, redemption and the cross

The kind of transformation that can enable redemptive relationships comes through a process of conversion akin to that evoked by the Christian gospel. Salvation begins with exposure and judgement. On the cross Christ sharpened the judgement, showing up the pride and self-confidence of religious people who thought they were doing God's will in getting rid of him, the compromise of a Pilate who was only doing his job in trying to keep the peace in the most notoriously turbulent province of the Empire, the weakness of friends who turned and ran, betrayed and denied . . . Here was a *krisis*, a moment of judgement in which people, both individuals and institutions, were shown up for what they really were. Christ sharpened the judgement and bore the consequences.

Judgement and wrath are deeply written into the biblical material. In the New Testament epistles (such as 1 Peter and Hebrews) suffering is a testing, a discipline, a kind of refinement. Paul at the beginning of Romans suggests that the wrath of God is at work in judging the sins and follies of humanity: they are given up to reap the consequences of their own actions. The creation was subjected to futility, he suggests later. It's only through the groaning and travailing, the submission to judgement, that salvation can come. The early Christians saw their own suffering under persecution, and the death of Christ on the cross, as a bearing of the final woes of judgement before the coming of God's kingdom.

Judgement and wrath are the other side of love's coin. There's no mercy without justice, no love without demand and expectation. Love expects loyalty, love sets standards, passionately wants the best *of* the loved one, as well as *for* him or her. Standards mean judgement, testing, criticism – these are part of love. Love must speak the truth, even if it be in judgement and anger. When a relationship breaks down, a cover-up does nothing to restore relations – only the anger of the offended party, the repentance of the offender, the offering and acceptance of reparation as a token of reconciliation and forgiveness can recreate it. If that is true in human relations, how much more in our relationship with God! Judgement is the reverse side of redemption's coin because only exposure of the truth can bring the fruits of repentance and the possibility of change. The religious experience of the saints suggests that the deeper you know God, the more aware you become of a kind of pollution, inadequacy, the more you sense that even the greatest moral achievements of human beings are somehow tainted, ambiguous. 'Take me away, and in the lowest deep there let me be,' sings Gerontius when he reaches God's presence. 'Woe is me; for I am a man of unclean lips and I dwell among a people of unclean lips,' cried Isaiah. He and his people are caught up together in a kind of pollution – judgement shouldn't be seen simply in individualistic terms. Live coals purge Isaiah's lips, and he's sent out with a message of judgement.

The trouble with judgement is that it so easily gets trapped in the law courts. The most widespread understanding of the cross, found among both Evangelicals and Catholics, exploits that analogy: humanity stands in the dock and should be condemned for its sin, but Christ steps in and takes the punishment on our behalf. Christ died for our sins, punished in our stead to satisfy the demands of divine justice. You can understand why this is powerful – it's part of my own evangelical experience to sense the joy and freedom of realizing that responsibility for one's actions has been lifted, that guilt at failure to live up to the demands and ideals of the gospel is resolved, amazement at the gift of grace. Besides it fits with one of the profoundest insights of Christian theology, namely the reality of sin – the pride and self-sufficiency of humanity which collectively and individually challenges and denies God, boasts of its own achievements, refuses to submit. That God cannot overlook or shrug off the sinful state of humankind must be true – love, true love, is not sentimental and soppy, but demanding as well as accepting. The necessity of judgement is respected.

Yet the very use of the law-court analogy undermines this as an acceptable theory of atonement. The theory has a moral and legal basis. So you would expect it to be morally and legally satisfactory. But is it? Can the substitution of an innocent victim for the guilty party do anything to satisfy the claims of justice, at least as we usually understand it? Why should a criminal get off scot-free while someone else gets the punishment? That kind of substitution would be a gross travesty of justice against which we would all protest in any other context.

Then there are theological problems. Isn't it the case that a concept of abstract justice actually determines the whole operation? And I mean *determines*. God's freedom has been lost; God's been bound by a principle. Why couldn't God just choose to be merciful? After all, even earthly kings can do that. The concept of God implied here is not consistent with the God of grace preached in the evangelical revival, nor with the God of sovereign freedom appealed to by Paul. And the difficulties don't end there. The Father is characterized as just and wrathful, and the Son as merciful and loving, voluntarily bearing in our stead the punishment inflicted by the Father. Such a doctrine is entirely out of tune with the consistent message of the New Testament: there salvation comes to humankind through God's initiative, and we find Christ acting on God's behalf even in judgement.

To those classic objections I find I need to add another. If that is the fundamental meaning of the gospel, what would salvation be for someone like Arthur? In what sense can he be said to be a sinner needing forgiveness, given such extreme limitations that he can hardly be held accountable for his actions or responses, let alone be expected to receive grace through faith? Maybe it makes a lot more sense simply to see the cross as a demonstration of God's love, the reaction of so-called Liberal Protestants: repentance comes from contemplation of the cross, and love is generated in us in response to God's love shown in Jesus Christ – for 'greater love has no one than this that he lay down his life for his friends'. But this kind of view drastically oversimplifies the very complex statements made about the meaning of the cross in the New Testament. The language of sacrifice and ransom, justification and redemption, is taken in a very much weakened sense. Besides, if the cross made no real difference, if it didn't establish a different relationship between God and humanity, why was it necessary? The resolution of guilt needs more than a loving demonstration that hurt doesn't matter. For, 'justice is the structural form of love without which it would be sheer sentimentality'.[13] Respect is lost on both sides if offences are shrugged off. It's all too wishy-washy, not least because it ignores the importance of judgement.

For me a family incident provided a parable which goes some way to doing justice to the concerns of both traditional theories while taking account of such objections. Our youngest, aged about eight, came home from school with a friend and they disappeared down the back garden. Some time later I discovered to my horror that they'd been throwing stones and had broken the window of a derelict-looking stable across the neighbour's fence. An old couple had a flat in that loft and the stones had been bouncing across the carpet of their living room. So what was needed to resolve the situation and re-establish neighbourly relations? Obviously the boy needed to appreciate the wrong he'd done, and had to apologize in person. But I, as parent, needed to make restitution on his behalf by replacing the broken window. Besides, together we needed to offer a gift, a box of chocolates and a bunch of flowers, to restore relations. In other words, wrongdoing had to be acknowledged and confessed, and reparation had to be made, even if the perpetrator, unable to do it for himself, needed someone to do it for him. So Christ died for our sins, offering reparation on our behalf. The atonement he offers in love for us we may then make our own, responding in love and thanksgiving. Like the sacrifices of old, like the blood given by God upon the altar to make atonement and restore life (Lev. 17.11), it was an offering made to deal with our sin.

Yet this whole approach to atonement offers a very moralistic and individualistic gospel. The question remains: what relevance has it to Arthur? Isn't he so limited as to be as innocent as a baby? Taking seriously the idea that we're all in it together might make a difference: as a member of the human race and embodied in human community, Arthur may be implicated in our corporate 'falling short of God's glory'. But another question also remains: how does that insight into the cross which Arthur provoked (and which was outlined in Chapter 2) connect with these theories? To answer that we need to broaden horizons on the human predicament and the saving work of Christ.

In 1996 I was involved in ecumenical dialogue on reconciliation at the Theological Faculty of the Serbian Orthodox Church in Belgrade under the auspices of the Conference of European Churches. My presentation on 'Reconciliation in a Theological Dimension' focused on Christ's work of atonement, by which we are reconciled with God. Later, in a small group discussion, an Orthodox priest commented, 'I really don't know about this atonement.' It was a salutary reminder that the saving work of Christ has been perceived very differently in much of Christian history, in Eastern Christianity particularly. The New Testament and the ancient traditions of the Church have many different ways of speaking of the cross, but they all resolve themselves into a single basic conception: a cosmic battle between good and evil, God and Satan, in which the cross was the decisive moment of victory. Salvation was liberation from a world possessed by demons, the destruction of sorcery and magic, ignorance and superstition, the conquest of sin and death, the end of mental and physical corruption. This was achieved by rescuing humanity from the clutches of Satan, a rescue effected by the cross as Christ conquered death and enabled a new creation.

Now this hardly seems relevant to those who find the idea of the devil and cosmic battles impossible to stomach outside science fiction (see Chapter 2). But we still face the problem of 'gone-wrongness'. Moral progress has not, in fact, gone in step with material and scientific progress. We're trapped in the 'total nexus of evil' in the world – the political, social and economic forces that bind us, our own heredity and environment, our own unconscious drives and the 'system'. Violence and injustice are institutionalized. Individuals get caught up in social and economic conflicts almost unawares. They're sucked into mass movements which effect destruction and spread hate. We're responsible, yet not responsible. We fashion the structures of society, yet are enslaved by them. There's a kind of demonic power evident in society and in history – indeed, within ourselves, even if we are sceptical about the devil.

Furthermore, the human predicament is not just a moral one, as Western approaches to atonement tend to assume. Something in the present constitution of creation as a whole has 'gone-wrong'. Sin is but one symptom of this deeper problem – in early Christianity other symptoms were identified as ignorance, weakness and sheer powerlessness; perversity and corruptibility; sickness, decay and death. Salvation is inseparable from the total problem of evil – indeed, the gospel is the solution to the problem of evil, if not in theory, at least in practice. Traditionally the cross is a symbol of triumph – a banner under which the Church continued the fight against all forms of evil – idolatry, heresy, sorcery, sin and, above all, death. The martyr and the monk forsook all to engage in the battle on the side of Christ, trusting that effective victory was already won by Christ's triumph on the cross. Now to reclaim this ancient approach to the cross enables us to reconnect with the insight given through Arthur's disability and the Gospel of John, to see that the cross is indeed about God confronting and redeeming the whole complex of 'gone-wrongness' that somehow afflicts the creation, not just sin but sickness and suffering, disability and death, not just the moral failures of individuals but the whole corporate mess we human beings have made of things, compounding the pain and suffering of the human predicament.

But we cannot abandon the notion of judgement. Suppose a kind of double reparation is made on the cross. On the one hand, God takes responsibility for the mess we protest against, offering reparation for creating a world like this, giving up the only begotten Son to suffer the consequences of all the 'gone-wrongness' of which we accuse the Creator, the suffering and the sin, the pain and purposeless devastation – for all of which God admits responsibility. On the other hand, the man Jesus, by his complete sacrifice of obedience unto death, offers reparation on our behalf, and invites us to take advantage of this, to receive the amnesty God offers, the overlooking of past sin that righteousness may be effected in us through the new covenant written on hearts ... For this restoration of relationship the structures of obligation have to be met, the responsibility of each party respected, judgement and anger expressed and acknowledged for change to be possible. The cross acts as judgement, exposing the sins of humankind which put Christ to death, and the anger of God against sin which Jesus had to brave on our behalf. Only the God-Man could bear it all.

Salvation comes through judgement. The resolution of the 'gone-wrongness' of humankind requires its exposure. In John's Gospel the deepest sin is disclosed as a kind of 'false consciousness' which fails to respond when confronted with the presence of one truly representing God. In that story of the healing of the blind man, the Pharisees end up asking, 'Are we also blind?' Jesus indicates that their sin is evident in the very fact that they claim to see. This surely throws light on the meaning of the saying about the unforgivable sin (Mark 3.21–30): what is this sin against the Holy Spirit? Well, the scribes have just accused Jesus of casting out demons by the power of Beelzebub, the principal demon. They are so spiritually blind that they mistake the Spirit of God for the spirit of evil. Such blindness cannot be forgiven precisely because they're sure they're right, so they'll never repent. Forgiveness can only be received if the offender is prepared to climb down. To climb down in this case would mean a radical change in fundamental outlook. The racist is blind to the sin of his/her attitude, but judgement takes place. Those who commit disability hate crimes are blind to the sin of their attitude, but judgement takes place. Those who pass by on the other side and cannot embrace those with disabilities are judged and need redemption. And this redemption is not something we can achieve for ourselves, try as we will. It's no good just feeling we ought to be able to respond in a certain way and desperately trying to bury our feelings. It doesn't work. It takes a miracle of grace for many of us to accept people as they are. So disability sharpens the judgement and tests our faith. There's a sense in which we can *do* nothing about it. There's no magic wand. But the way we handle it is crucial for the creation of true human values and true human community. It provides a constant living parable of human frailty, but also of its potential transcendence through the grace of God. The love of God is a love which is searing like live coals, for our own good. It's purging and painful, searching out the hidden contamination of sin to which we like to close our eyes. For 'the word of God is living and active, sharper than any two-edged sword, piercing until it divides soul from spirit, joints from marrow', and 'able to judge the thoughts and intentions of the heart' (Heb. 4.12). It was the pain of that judgement that Christ bore on the cross. He took it upon himself. That is what atonement is about – the bearing of the pain of judgement in love.

In conclusion: redemptive suffering

Christianity has always claimed that suffering is redemptive, and that the cross of Christ in particular is the means of salvation – hence *Good* Friday. Often the word sacrifice is called in to explain these notions. From the beginning such ideas intrigued me – indeed, sacrifice was the subject of my doctoral thesis and my first published book, *Sacrifice and the Death of Christ*, which took the research findings and sought to tease out in a more popular way their relevance today. It was subsequently that the cross began to resolve for me the questions arising from Arthur's situation – indeed the general issues of theodicy – by providing what I saw as the truly Christian answer to modern anxiety around the problem of evil and suffering: God, challenged to justify the awful things that happen in God's own creation, is revealed there on the cross as taking responsibility for all that 'gone-wrongness' by entering and bearing it all in the person of Jesus Christ. This approach, however, was in some ways to turn the traditional understanding of the cross on its head. From the New Testament on, Christianity proclaimed that Christ died, not for God's mistakes or failures, but for *our sins*. Further reflection on sin and judgement, to some extent provoked by the ambiguous reactions of people to those with disabilities, alongside insight into the Scriptures, revealed that sin and suffering are not altogether disconnected, and alike belong to that 'gone-wrongness' which it was God's initiative to put right, offering a double reparation to restore relationships. Thus the cross became the atoning sacrifice to end all sacrifices.

In our common parlance, to make a sacrifice is to give something up, and giving it up is something that hurts – the ultimate sacrifice is giving up one's life for some cause, such as the defence of one's country. In the societies surrounding the Bible and early Christianity, however, sacrifice was always to do with worship, and fundamentally it signified gifts to the gods: offerings made sacred in liturgy. Gifts in ordinary life have all kinds of meanings depending on context and intention: they're offered to celebrate a birthday, to say 'thank you' or to say 'sorry', and so on. Basically the same was true of sacrificial offerings. Sometimes sacrifices expressed thanksgiving for benefits received, sometimes tribute given to worship and honour the divine Lord; sometimes they accompanied repayment of debt, or were offered as a bribe; sometimes they reinforced a plea for mercy, or were a desperate attempt to placate anger. Sometimes offerings were made to hostile spirits, to keep them away. Often communal sacrifices were a way of celebration, a bit like an anniversary or a birthday party, everyone offering gifts and sharing a feast together in communion with the divinity. Although early Christians rejected the practice of sacrifice, sacrificial language was applied to the cross, as well as to the Eucharist. The question I explored in research for my thesis was exactly what was meant by this application. The answer with respect to the Eucharist appears relatively easy – the word means 'thanksgiving', and it's clearly a communion feast. But when it comes to understanding the sacrificial meaning of the cross, it's all a bit trickier, and because, as a memorial of the death of Christ, the Eucharist is closely associated with the cross, that too is not so simple as it looks.

Just as I couldn't believe in a devil of a God who would punish me for some misdeed or other with a child like Arthur, so I could never believe that the cross was a sacrifice to propitiate or placate God's wrath, or to buy off God's punishment. A few early Christians played around with that kind of idea, but actually found themselves embarrassed by it – after all, it was God the Father who'd sent the Son into the world to redeem it, and to imagine Son set against Father, or vice versa, was to undermine the oneness of the Trinity. Early theologians agreed that Christ made an offering of perfect human obedience to God, but mostly Christ's death on the cross was seen as a ransom offered to free humankind from Satan's clutches. Alongside that picture, the biblical view (Lev. 17.11) that God's mercy provided the blood of sacrifice as a way of atonement, to deal with sin, purify and sanctify, was taken as fulfilled through the offering of the blood of Christ, as suggested in the Epistle to the Hebrews. Fifty years on, I recently found further confirmation of this for early Christianity: one monastic preacher noted that 'in the Law irrational animals were offered in sacrifice, and unless they were slain, they were not acceptable as offerings'. 'Now,' he continued, 'unless sin is slain the offering is not acceptable to God, nor is it authentic.'[14] The nub of his homily was that no one can perform this sacrifice for themselves; God alone can purify the soul's sordidness, wash it and give it life. So the cross understood as sacrifice was all about dealing with sins, something God undertook to do on our behalf.

The reflections in this chapter suggest that the idea of sacrifice needs to be returned to its primary context, namely worship and liturgy: the sacred place where ritual plays out the dynamics of humankind's fraught relationship with the Creator and Father of all. Ultimately the sacrifice of Christ on the cross is not about a legal transaction, but about the kind of love that exposes the truth about our moral ambiguities, about the way our very virtues may be the germ of our worst faults, the kind of love that stays with our pain, with the anguish of hearts before the inexplicable mysteries of life, with the suffering of innocents, with the absence of resolution in the face of tragedy. That 'staying with' rather than 'putting right' is a perception deepened by living with irremovable disability. The persistence of the marks of the nails on the resurrected body of Christ is a sign of God's commitment to be in it with us, and by solidarity with us God in Christ enables suffering borne in love or innocence to become itself redemptive through communion with Christ's redemptive suffering. The hope signified is that the darkest compost from the least wanted weeds is the most fertile, and the cross on which we perceive God sharing our God-forsakenness becomes the tree of life blossoming with the fruits of the Spirit. I thank God that Arthur has thus been the catalyst for deepening insights into this, the very heart of the gospel of Christ.

6

Loving and letting go

————•◆•————

At Faith and Light's twentieth-anniversary celebration in Russia (see Chapter 3) I was asked to meet with parents each day, while their children (many adult) were engaged in activities with friends and helpers. Through an interpreter they kept asking their questions, and my most vivid memory is of their anguished repetition of the same basic concern: 'What's going to happen to my son/daughter when I die?' Or 'What about when I can no longer care for him/her?' Russia still has large institutions, and everyone was terrified of that being the only future. Anxiety fizzed through the room, and what could I say? I could empathize, I could speak of trust in God, I could quote St Julian of Norwich: 'All will be well, all manner of things will be well' – but what reassurance was that, given the harsh realities, not to mention my own long struggle with the same basic question? Maybe it had been helpful in the early days to feel that Arthur would always need me, but as the long term stretched into ever longer term, how would it be?

Little did I realize it at the time but within less than a year we'd be confronted with the need to resolve that same issue. In Russia I already had what proved to be tendonitis in my right hand, and it would be 18 months or so before the problem was finally resolved. For two months in the winter of 2010–11 my physiotherapist insisted that I shouldn't use that hand, so Bob became Arthur's sole carer. Then I became the sole carer after Bob had a cataract operation. No sooner were we through that than sudden acute pain in Bob's leg, exacerbated by getting Arthur up one morning, meant that we were reduced to one carer again. We'd always said things were fine as long as we could box-and-cox, but we'd now had several months in which one or other of us was out of action, putting considerable physical strain on the other. A weekend visit from one of our sons put the question of Arthur's future on the table while I was out leading a service in a local Methodist church. I was suddenly confronted with it on my return, already feeling a bit drained. I was shattered, and none of those inadequate platitudes I'd offered to other mothers in Russia could touch my anguish. The practical struggles of the next year or so were compounded by insomnia and emotional stress. I knew with my head it had to happen, but my heart couldn't bear the thought of losing Arthur.

Loss and grief

To my shame, at least in hindsight, the grief was all too self-oriented. I was in the midst of preparation for a major series of theological lectures which were to bring together historical research and my personal reflections on life, particularly the ways in which Arthur had given me privileged insight into the historic claims of Christian theology. So my first reaction was that I was losing my credentials. In the event that loss was far from imminent – it would take over a year for Social Services to come up with funding and authorize the search for a suitable placement. Meanwhile, apropos those credentials, my old minister and mentor Chris Hughes Smith said, 'Maybe he's done his job!' In any case that first reaction was superficial compared with the reality. The prospect felt like bereavement, and it was compounded by all that Arthur had come to mean to me. As Jean Vanier would put it, Arthur had become my gateway to God – little wonder that the loss was so deeply personal. Yet, as in the early years (see Chapter 1), I was held together by inexorable demands: physically I had to keep going, taking over more of the domestic pressures as well as Arthur's care; spiritually I was still regularly leading worship, accompanied by Arthur; mentally I had to prepare to deliver those lectures and then polish the material for publication. My final emergence from two years of anguish would in the end be related to the production of that publication. That is a story for later but helps with perspective as I look back on the grieving process.

For in retrospect I can see how the intense reaction of grief meant that I lost what wisdom I'd gained over the years. Once I'd understood that love means letting go, that it was good to let others care for Arthur, to accept respite care, to rejoice that Arthur had a life of his own and knew people I didn't know. During those years after Bob took early retirement and I was preoccupied with my professional life, I had to a fair extent been 'weaned off' him, though still engaged in practice, most nights feeding him and putting him to bed. For many years things had been on an even keel, and once my mother was living with us, Arthur and Granny were such good companions I knew we should not do anything to upset that. The future was in the background, though sometimes, for his sake, I would secretly pray that he would pre-decease us and we'd never have to make a decision about his future, especially when we were faced with his patches of distress. A scary incident when he had a fit in the bath and slipped under the water cured me of that: thinking I had lost him, I knew that wasn't what I wanted. Indeed, after retirement, I'd gradually become less relaxed and once again excessively anxious about his ups and downs – the attachment became more obsessive. When faced with losing him to residential care this all came to an emotional head. I would eventually have to learn that I needed him more than he needed me: a painful lesson. The grief was all too self-oriented.

I guess too there was an element of now feeling the depths of cumulative loss over many years. Arthur's life had been a series of losses, to which we'd responded as positively as possible. His condition, once diagnosed, meant the loss of normal parental expectations, but we'd ridden his childhood with determination that he'd gain as much development as possible, only to experience the loss of what we'd gained, particularly in mobility, during his early adult years. So physically he'd long been deteriorating, and some years before this he'd even lost his beautiful hair. He may not have appreciated his own situation, but I grieved for him, and the years of suppressed grief no doubt surfaced in those months of waiting for his future to be resolved.

For, yes – concern for him was a major contributing factor to my grief, particularly as it became clear that he was going to lose everything he knew. He would not only lose his home and his parental carers, he would lose the well-known and regular respite care at Kingswood, and eventually it emerged that once Social Services was funding his residential care, they wouldn't continue to fund his place at the Day Centre. So his weekday routine of 25 years or more was also going. His whole life was being turned upside down, with its familiar landmarks removed. And that undoubtedly exacerbated my anxiety. I simply wanted desperately to be able to make everything right for him, while feeling I was losing control. We'd eventually get some reassurance from the Day Centre manager – she confirmed that once in residential care, Arthur would not be able to continue attendance; but she also said that she used to worry about the effect of such disruptions on clients, only to discover they usually took such changes in their stride. This would certainly prove to be the case with Arthur, but it was hard to believe it in advance.

Of course, it didn't help that during those months the scandal at Winterbourne View hit the news media. Terrible footage of carers abusing persons with learning disabilities kept being replayed on the television. How could I find a quite fundamental trust in the future, and believe that people would value not abuse him? But even without that, there was part of me that questioned the meaning of Arthur's life when he'd have lost his entire context and all his existing relationships. How could I be confident that his life would have meaning when everything he knew (home, family, Kingswood, Day Centre) was taken from him? Was it possible to reach a recognition that his existence and quality of life was not my sole responsibility, that he would belong somewhere to somebody, if not to me? Meanwhile, I vowed to enjoy him while I'd got him. I began to celebrate the little interactions, the smiles and the clapping, to take time embracing him and feeling his arms around my shoulders as he clung on when lifting him out of his wheelchair. That helped to ease the constant demands, to defuse the guilt arising from a crying need for relief, a need which just complicated the anguish at imminent loss.

If I'm honest, however, the grief at losing Arthur was compounded by other levels of heartache as our lives changed. The situation challenged long-standing ways in which Bob and I lived and worked as a team. Besides, it was occasioned by our own bodily 'wear-and-tear', signs that our lives would become constrained by the inevitable losses that come with ageing. It was not because of Arthur that we had to forgo our annual adventure, cycling and camping in France – the usual respite care was available, but by then Bob was awaiting knee surgery. At times of stress and anxiety, even minor disappointments tend to gain excessive weight. The grief seemed to shift around and fasten itself on one thing after another, whether large or small, twisting perspectives on hopes and fears, memories and relationships. Through the long lonely nights with insomnia, loss of Bob was foreshadowed in the loss of Arthur.

Looking back, however, I can see that this period of grief was significant in more ways than one. It became a *krisis* in the sense explored in the previous chapter, exposing deep-seated responses and feelings that I needed to deal with. I gradually reached greater self-understanding, and learned to have compassion on myself. I experienced again that deep connection between grief at significant loss or bereavement and heightened sensitivity to beauty, especially in nature and music. I realized how important it was to love others – Arthur, Bob, even God – more for themselves than for what they are for me. Indeed, I probably prayed more in the long night watches than at other periods of my life. Certain friends with whom I conversed may remember how I became obsessed with the figure of Jesus, longing to find a way of relating to him, not just as the one who entered our darkness on the cross and transformed it into light, but as the human friend alongside. Somehow I needed a face to relate to, but the traditional Sunday school picture of Jesus with fair hair and blue eyes simply failed – Jesus was a Jew of the Middle East. I found an El Greco depiction of a dark Mediterranean Jesus, but it was again a Jesus carrying the cross. Eventually I rediscovered the Coptic icon I'd brought back from Moscow – there were those large eyes looking at me, and the hand of friendship on my shoulder. Of course, even a mental image of Christ's face would be an idol. But an icon is not to be taken literally – it's a representation which enables a sense of presence. In my reclusive 'hermit's cave', tied by being Arthur's only carer and racked by grief and loss, I lived through lonely struggles with myself, eventually to receive deeper grace. Slowly it became possible to embrace a kind of communal solitude, to catch sight of the possibility of deeper intercessory identification with humanity, a sense of praying the Church's prayer and sharing in the communion of saints. Yet this coexisted with a massive loss of faith and trust – in other people, in God. For what was this grief but a failure to believe that I could entrust Arthur to others or leave the future in God's hands?

I knew what I needed was a fundamental shift, away from this overwhelming sense of loss, away from desperate attempts to envisage and accept the unknown future, to positive anticipation of new possibilities, to hope that out of letting go could come greater riches. The Gospels speak of denying oneself to receive life (Mark 8.34–35), and of Jesus going away so that greater things could happen (John

14.12) – was something like that possible? Now and then glimmers of hope surfaced, and precious moments offered relief. I heard a 'loud thought': 'Let go, let me take care of him.' One Sunday I found myself joining in that chorus, 'Because he lives I can face tomorrow'; I wonder if you've ever noticed the verse about the newborn baby? 'Greater still the calm assurance: this child can face uncertain days because he lives.' But final resolution would take much longer than I realized.

Meanwhile, with much distress, in May 2011 I signed Arthur's life away. Peter and Mary Humble were staying for a few days, helping in the garden with the dahlias which Bob now had problems planting. The social worker called with the necessary papers all finally completed. I signed. He left. I wept. It would be another year before Arthur actually left home, and almost a further year before I finally emerged from my tunnel. But now I can look back and say it with flowers:

> Rage, rage at the dying of the light.
> Weep at losses that punctuate life.
> But no – no longer, not any more.
>
> For delicate purple cranes-bill blooms
> Peek out from summer's straggling verge
> Of downy thistle and willow-herb,
> Of ragwort, mugwort and meadowsweet,
> Of wild carrot skeletons, bramble and burrs,
> The burnished bronze of dying docks
> And yellow grass fronds gone to seed,
> Where nightshade lurks and autumn's approach
> Turns traveller's joy to old man's beard.
>
> Yes – cranes-bill petals of purple silk
> Join cornflower florets spreading wide,
> Their knapweed cousins luring bees,
> As pink little flutes of bindweed climb
> The straggle of nettles past their best.
> By teasels and tansies and trumpets of white
> Convolvulus, elder, hips and haws
> Now bear the promise of berry fruits.
>
> Weep not for the promise of loss is gain.
> Rage not. At the tunnel's end is light.

Letting go

The signing of those papers was but the beginning. The case had to be referred to the community nurse for assessment, and more form-filling. As she had to work to a defined timetable, we believed that things would be moving by the autumn, but then there were endless delays, and further questions about how Arthur's complex needs would be met in a typical care home. The funding was finally agreed in March 2012, and we cannot help but deduce that the deciding issue was the beginning of a new financial year. One of my reflections over this period was the gap between our actual day-to-day coping and the need to present a catalogue of needs and difficulties to get any assistance or progress with the case. I had to keep pushing for something that at a deeper level I really didn't want. When someone commented, 'That's a terrible decision you've had to make', my eyes were opened to the reality that deep down I felt I'd not made the decision – it'd been thrust upon me. I realized I needed to make it my own or I'd never be able to move on.

When the funding finally came through the social worker said that some of the money could be used to assist us in caring for him while the process of identifying his future home was under way. But in the event nothing happened. What we requested was regular help to bath him, but since we have no hoisting facilities upstairs, no agency would supply the help we requested. It's typical that parents and friends manage all kinds of things care workers are not allowed to do, or cannot get insurance for: from time to time I still cut his nails and trim his moustache when he's at home on a visit – scissors can prove too much of a risk! One step we had taken during this period was to change the car; with Bob out of action I simply couldn't go on lifting Arthur out of his wheelchair into the front seat of our Galaxy every time it was needed. Our neighbour had noticed my struggles on one occasion, and mentioned it to Bob. At first it seemed the wrong moment to get a vehicle adapted for wheelchairs, when Arthur was about to leave home; but then we realized that we'd still want to take him out, or bring him home for visits, even after he no longer lived with us. It's made a huge difference to be able to push Arthur up the ramp and secure his wheelchair in the back of a converted Fiat Doblo, though I don't think he gets such a good view as we drive along. Never mind – now things are more back to normal for us the car is a wonderful cycle-carrier when Arthur isn't with us.

So with the funding secured, finding Arthur's new home was the next stage. We were invited to view a few homes with vacancies, though our choice would have to be agreed by the social worker and community nurse, who would check that appropriate care could be provided there. Points of contact became problematic for a while since the social worker had weeks away on compassionate leave, but one way and another over a couple of months we were given four possible homes to consider. We met a range of impressive people in the process, and beginning to see places where Arthur might be, and meet people who might become his carers, certainly made me feel better about it all. It was the last home we visited which immediately became our first choice. As we left, I said, 'That's the nearest we've seen to a L'Arche foyer.'

Tucked in behind old houses, the little purpose-built bungalow for six residents was away from the busy street and surrounded by big trees with its own patch of quiet garden – all perfect for Arthur, especially the little conservatory with its Venetian blinds! Patterns of light and shade have always fascinated him – grilles, blinds, wooden fences, tree-skeletons in winter. Belonging to a housing association, the home had been established when Monyhull Hospital was being closed, had been run by the NHS for seven years, but for the past two years had been managed by a charity. Currently they had two vacancies. We sat round the dining table with the staff on duty, many of whom had been working there for years – a fellow-parent had primed us to ask about staff turnover. Two of the residents were capable of indicating what a good place it was to live, and the atmosphere felt friendly and positive. We learned that staff took some residents to the church on the old Monyhull campus on Sunday mornings, as well as going out shopping with them, taking them for a regular session in the sensory room at Moseley Day Centre, and having a weekly visit from the music man (see Introduction). We left knowing we'd found the right place, and checking the CQC website confirmed that this had the best score of the homes we'd been able to see. Quickly we registered our interest.

Now the manager of the home, Denise, had to make her own assessment. She came for a meal with us, saw how we fed and handled Arthur, and discussed all the health issues – the potential pressure sores, the scoliosis, the epilepsy. She thanked us for choosing her home and was very reassuring. At a later stage, when we were finally letting go, though my anxiety was evident as I confessed, 'He's still my baby', she simply said, 'Think of it as extended respite care.' That was the most helpful thing anyone managed to say, and I shall always be grateful for a remark which tied this new stage to long-standing experience of periods living without him.

After all the months of delay, suddenly things started to move fast. The Day Centre was to be closed for the week of the double bank holiday at the beginning of June 2012. Denise suggested that Arthur should go over to what would be his new home each day to try it out. So, a few days after his forty-fifth birthday, I took him there in the car, and stayed with him for about four hours. Michelle, one of the carers, took a delight in feeding him chocolate mousse, and that was the start of what is clearly an important relationship – a deep fondness. For the rest of the week Arthur was there from about 10 a.m. to 7 p.m., and their minibus was used to fetch him and return him, except for the last morning when it was needed for something else. I shall never forget driving Arthur over there that Friday; as I turned into the drive, I heard him chuckle in the back of the car. He was already recognizing the place and pleased to be going there.

The next week he was back to the old routine at the Day Centre, but it turned out to be his last week. On Friday afternoon we went there for his farewell party. People were all over him, and he was clearly a bit edgy and overwhelmed by it all. The following Monday his special bed and mattress (supplied by the district nurse service) was moved three miles across the city, and he left home. It had happened, and it all seemed rather sudden. For the first few weeks, anxiety was softened by sheer relief, and an unexpected sense of how utterly exhausted I'd become. There had been a slow wearing down, physical and psychological, for 18 months or so, and I finally admitted that it felt like the lifting of a burden, even if that burden had been made light by all that Arthur had come to mean. It's true that after recovering from the knee operation Bob had again been able to assist for a bit, but then a shoulder problem had been exacerbated by an accident and once again all the pressure was on me. Now I remembered Jesus' saying: 'Come to me, all who labour and are heavy laden, and I will give you rest' (Matt. 11.28, RSV), and I began to accept this gift of time and space, even to start thinking about joining a choir the following autumn. Meanwhile we planned a brief holiday before an operation on Bob's shoulder.

Adjusting

It was truly amazing how Arthur settled to the place. As the Day Centre manager had predicted, he took the move in his stride. I began to reflect that our roles were reversing – like mountaineers we were roped together for life, but he was going to lead me into this new world. For if he's happy, I must learn to be happy, too. Once again we began to think that though he clearly recognizes people and places he perhaps doesn't have much recall, and so doesn't miss them. After a couple of months the staff began to comment that they thought he was missing me, but I confess I was a bit sceptical. Once when I called in, however, he'd not been himself and was resting in bed. As soon as he saw me, he dissolved into tears, and so did I. Occasionally, even a year and more later, they report that he's missed me, or had a tearful spell, so perhaps we underestimate him. But maybe it's a blessing that he's so limited in his understanding – I guess it's made it a much easier transition.

Gradually Arthur has had to accept new patterns and routines. I get the impression that he really appreciates not having to be rushed up in the morning to go to the Day Centre – and I confess we 'old uns' have got lazy in the morning, too. Whereas we used to look at each other at breakfast and say, 'We still have a job to do' (see Chapter 1), now we really feel retired and often, for breakfast, we're in our dressing gowns! For Arthur the most notable change has been the loss of time each day on his beanbag. Denise had to get his care plan approved by various advisers, and there were too many risks for carers in getting him on to it and back into his wheelchair, particularly as it was so large that the legs of their little hoist wouldn't go around it without someone lifting its corners. Now he has a routine of spending time on his bed during the afternoon to get a break from the chair. In the early days Denise and others were excited to find that he'd dance on the bed to videos of Michael Jackson. He's been given his own TV and other sensory stimulants, lights and music; and there's always the old favourite hammer. Sometimes he's been there on his bed when I've visited. On one occasion he was asleep, and as I sat beside him, he gradually woke and recognized me, with a little edge of emotion and more and more response, till he was saying, 'Oh, Arthur' and 'Mummy' in his own inimitable way, allowing me to embrace him, to interact with mutual 'head-banging' and smiles; then eventually he pushed me away, and later showed no reaction to my 'Bye-bye' – that's OK, he seemed to be saying, he'd seen me, and now this was his place.

The truly amazing thing is that very quickly the staff got Arthur drinking again, on a more or less a regular basis – it was something we'd struggled with, especially in the last few years. Once when visiting, and nothing was right with Arthur till he'd had a drink and his lunch, I found myself thinking, 'I don't know this boy'; Bob regards his drinking as a real triumph on their part. Soon they were reporting on the different drinks he liked, as well as his response to going out into the community. They took him shopping and changed the character of his wardrobe. When he received his own personal invitation to his brother's wedding they began to talk about getting him a suit. And sure enough, the following July he did indeed have a smart suit, with a shirt to match the lining, and a neat bow-tie – the only problem being that the weather was far too hot to put the jacket on. And even though he lost the beanbag Arthur gained in other ways: Denise got a grant to get a special sling on which he could safely sit all day in his wheelchair without it exacerbating his pressure sore problem. She also arranged for a review of his special, shaped seating. Arthur's new carers have continued to ask us to help give him familiar company and assurance when things like hospital appointments have come up, so that was a process where his dad came into his own – he'd always been the one to cope with Arthur on the often distressing journey from initial seat mould to trying out the new support.

Over the past months there've been precious moments in which I've been able to catch a glimpse of Arthur's new life and relationships. There was the day Val came over to talk, and spoke of how sometimes she comes into work in the morning feeling all down, and then she goes in to Arthur, and he lifts his head from the pillow, and suddenly his smile is an answer to prayer. I know all about that – coming in from a demanding day at work and finding that Arthur ministered to me. But the fact that Val found the same thing gave me an answer to that agonizing question I'd asked myself for so many months. Could I present him as a gift to others, as a sacrifice properly speaking, in other words, an offering given for the sake of others though at some cost to myself?

Indeed, Arthur's significance to his carers has been an immense consolation. There was the young man attached to Arthur as an apprentice key worker; in a time of mass youth unemployment, Arthur was giving someone a future. There was the more experienced person first designated as his key worker, a Muslim whose life story I heard while Arthur was having dental treatment in theatre at the hospital. He'd grown up in Birmingham, a bit of a wild street-kid, and had had a wake-up call when caught up in a crazy driving escapade across the city. Wondering what he was doing with his life, he started going to the mosque, and then found himself when he discovered how people like Arthur responded to him; indeed, by then, for several months I'd watched Arthur chuckling whenever he approached. Proudly he told me of his NVQs, and I couldn't help recalling that 'wise saying' from our first meeting at L'Arche: 'My saviour is the one who needs me.' For various reasons those two moved on, but Arthur's next key worker, Max, seemed a quietly caring, reliable person whom I could not help trusting, and the same is true of Patrick – early on I watched him gently and respectfully encouraging Arthur to feed. Then there was Mohammed, the deputy manager, always helpful and considerate, and Nicole, and so many others.

Quickly I developed a regular pattern, with Arthur. At first I'd imagined it would be important to make the transition somewhat gradual. So with a grandson's help Bob got Arthur's old bed re-erected, and when he came home at the weekend he stayed overnight. But after relatively few occasions I was told that it seemed to unsettle him and he didn't sleep well the next night. Overnight stays were stopped, rather to my relief – suddenly the physical challenge of dressing and undressing and lifting had become heaps bigger, especially without the help of the hospital bed's adjustability. Yet it felt like an even more final moment.

Still, however, I retain the habit of picking him up most Sunday mornings to spend the day with us. First we go to church, sometimes to the place where I'm planned to lead worship as a minister, some-times to the old local Methodist church where he and his brothers grew up. He recognizes each one, having regularly been with me every Sunday for years, and people recognize him – if he's not with me for some reason I get anxious enquiries wherever I go. Then he comes home for a light lunch, an afternoon in familiar places, a period on his bed looking at the trees through the window, possibly some time in the garden. He watches *Songs of Praise* lying on the old beanbag with the old favourite hammer toy, has dinner with us and then goes back about 8 p.m. After about six weeks I caught myself saying, 'When I took Arthur home . . .' I suppose that signified a degree of acceptance on my part. There was a patch that first autumn when he protested at being put in the car in the evening, and inevitably I got anxious, but it seems likely that he simply wasn't used to going out after dinner in the dark, and the disturbance to routine upset him, especially if he'd been comfortably back on the beanbag. By the time we turned into the drive at his new home he was invariably chuckling, and then pushed me away as I tried to say 'Goodbye'. One evening he triumphantly said, '-ye-ye', as I pushed him towards the door, and that made me finally acknowledge that I needed him more than he needed me. It was far from easy to accept without tears, but he was becoming his own man.

Apart from Sundays at home I normally try to visit for an hour midweek. This seems particularly important for getting to know the other residents and the staff, as well as keeping in touch with how things are going for Arthur. I had always dreaded the thought of going to visit him in a home – you can't have a conversation with him, and our real contact had mostly been through feeding him and dressing him, with intermittent communication through clapping and imitative vocalizing as we got on with things around the house. Now I felt I had to find a new way of being with him. My big problem was that I felt the need to get some kind of interaction with him, and often he really didn't want to know. Before he left home I'd got him willingly to accept it if I put my arms around him, rested my head on his shoulder and gave him a kiss, while he put his arms round my shoulders. But at home this was most often the prelude to lifting him from his wheelchair when about to dress or change him, and away from home he just pushed me away – I wasn't part of his routine in this different place. Indeed it often felt as though he thought I didn't belong there. Of course, thinking about it, I realize he never saw me when staying at Kingswood, and rarely at the Day Centre; so he too must have found my visits to a context away from home a new experience. In some ways it's been easier to have physical contact with him when he's on the bed – on one occasion I managed to get him on my knee and share some real embraces; but that kind of contact has been rare. Mostly he hasn't wanted to know, yet my attachment to him drove me to keep attempting physical contact, looking for a response from him, and repeatedly hurt that he didn't seem to want me. I'd lost the wisdom to let go and let be. I needed him more than he needed me.

Recently I was reading a little book about a French film, *Les Intouchables* (*The Untouchables*) – reflections by Jean Vanier and others on this challenging film about disability and other marginalized people. There were many familiar comments – the importance of the 'other' for bringing about transformation, and the significance of touch, which 'far from implying sexuality should be the expression of acceptance of the other's fragility, and also of our own'. But what brought me up short was a story about Edith – surely the very Edith who had had such an impact on me (see Chapter 3). An assistant at L'Arche was persuaded of the importance of offering Edith gestures of tenderness when working with her, and was secretly vexed by what she took to be rejection. A colleague noticed and commented on the way she was handling Edith, how she hustled her when things took too long, how she failed to adapt her pace to the rhythm of Edith's needs. The assistant then began to notice her own body language, the little signs of impatience, and gradually realized how much her attempts at tenderness came from a kind of assumed concern. She spoke of an 'apprenticeship in patience', which paid off in remarkable ways as she was able to relax, not to renounce or disengage from her responsibilities, but to savour a new level of tenderness which began to establish itself between herself and Edith.

I realized that was a lesson I had to learn – to relax my urgency to relate to Arthur and stimulate his response, to respond myself to his rhythm; and that meant learning simply to be with him, watching, waiting, savouring silence. It's taken a year and more to get there, but I've been helped by Pat, one of the other residents, who is always willing to give me a hug when Arthur won't. At first it was easier to go along with others – visiting friends and family who came along to see where Arthur is now. The thing is, you can see him listening to our conversation, and you know he knows you're there, as he gently smiles and looks through his fingers. The same relaxed response comes from him if a resident or a staff member comes across to talk, but often they're busy and leave me to have 'quality time' with him – if only! Sometimes in summer he enjoys a walk around the garden looking at the trees; very occasionally he's enjoyed a game with my hat, or a cushion, or a ball; there may be some quiet interaction through clapping or vocalization, and there was one time when he tried to remove my specs – something he'd not done for years! They always bring me tea, and sometimes I'm able to offer him a drink. He once shared a piece of cake they'd brought me, and Michelle was surprised – she thought he'd only take cake with custard. At last, however, I'm learning the patience to wait, to recognize his little signs of response to my presence, and even at times to use the silence between us for reflection and prayer. But still there's an ache for his recognition, and deep gratitude when his chuckle greets me.

Arthur's first winter away from home was not without its ups and downs. Not long before he left home we'd seen his dentist – as ever over the years I was worried about his mouth as we struggled with his eating and drinking. It turned out that his gums were expanding over his teeth in places, and the dentist had raised the question whether it would be worth removing all his teeth, since he hardly chews efficiently and to do any treatment requires a general anaesthetic. My immediate reaction was, 'Yes, let's deal with it once and for all.' By the time the appointment for the operation came in the autumn the dentist was having second thoughts and I was increasingly anxious about the trauma involved. What settled it was the reluctance of the anaesthetist to put him to sleep outside a context where there would be full emergency back-up – Arthur's chest cavity was reduced by his worsening scoliosis. So it had to be rearranged for early in the new year, and by that time we were ready to agree that once the dentist could have a good look, he would decide what was best to do. In the end, encouraged by the readiness of the hospital anaesthetist to put Arthur to sleep again if necessary, he removed only a couple of teeth, did some fillings and sorted out the gums. Arthur recovered amazingly quickly, and was back eating and drinking quite normally within a week or so; but the whole episode, of course, heightened my anxiety.

And indeed, shortly after this, Arthur went into one of his patches of distress, never relaxed, constantly fussing, refusing everything. As ever, there was the frustration of not being able to find out what the problem was. I was able to confirm that this happened from time to time and almost always proved eventually to have some physical cause, such as a pressure sore or toothache – it wasn't just a behavioural problem. We'd had a rough time with him for several weeks the previous couple of winters: once he'd had a bout of flu, had been on antibiotics and then developed oral thrush (this had proved to be a recurring problem which could affect his eating and drinking); on other occasions pressure sores, either on his vulnerable hip or on the side of his foot, had left him uncomfortable whatever position he was in. The difficulty now was that he had a new GP and new district nurses, and I was only in contact with them via his new carers, who were all equally puzzled and struggling to get to the bottom of the problem. After about three weeks Arthur gradually emerged from this upset period. As this happened his new GP finally caught me on the phone, and we were able to have a long conversation about his history. We're none the wiser as to what caused this particular episode, but since then he's been his usual contented self, well settled to his new life.

As for me, during those weeks I was at one level grateful that this time it wasn't me struggling with him off and on for 24 hours a day, but the stress and anxiety mounted again, and revealed that I hadn't yet let go. In fact, part of the problem was not being in control, even though I no more had the solution than anyone else – indeed, sometimes when I visited I wondered if my presence only made things worse. I was still prone to tears, longing to put things right for him. Despite all the positives, this episode showed how far I still was from accepting, let alone celebrating, Arthur's new independent life; but, months later, that's exactly what I am able to do. And all because of the final breakthrough . . .

Lazarus, Arthur and Jesus

The story I have to tell bridges this whole period of letting go, and it's all about faces. Those lectures I was working on had picked up Jean Vanier's suggestion that Lazarus might have been a person with learning disabilities, and through Lazarus I was gradually brought face to face with Arthur, and with the Jesus I'd been searching for.

It began with meeting an artist who is also an icon-writer, Silvia Dimitrova. Most icons belong to carefully conserved traditions, but she was prepared to try creating for me an icon of the Lazarus which Jean Vanier described – the disabled brother, cared for by his sisters, in whose house he dwelt, and for whose sake they were unmarried. Work began the autumn after Arthur left home. I'd explained that I hoped that the figure of Lazarus would suggest my son. Silvia started with the question how to represent a wheelchair in icon style, and came up with the idea of copying the chariot from an icon of Elijah's ascent to heaven. The first sketch also included two typical features of an icon: the tree of life, leaning over and picking up the curve of the chariot wheels, and a house, behind a traditional figure of Jesus holding a Gospel book, his other hand lifted in blessing. Through conversation this was modified, so that Jesus leans over, with his hand on Lazarus' shoulder, creating an implicit circle with the existing curves of the wheels and the tree – a complete circle apart from the line of Jesus' back foot. In the iconographic tradition such a circle represents God's perfection, so here it's broken only by Christ stepping down to touch our lives. Thus, the composition, which has become the cover-image for the book of the lectures, took on layers of meaning. The chariot is not only a wheelchair but a box-like coffin from which the seated figure of Lazarus rises, as well as the symbol of heavenly ascent. The house is where Mary and Martha cared for Lazarus, yet also one of the 'many mansions' in 'my Father's house'. The tree is both the tree of life and a sign of Arthur's fascination with trees – and this became the more significant with the discovery that the words 'tree', 'true', 'trust', 'tryst' and 'betroth' are all etymologically related – while the childlike face and tonsured head of Lazarus elusively captures Arthur's look.

Some close friends have offered further responses to this unusual icon. One said she'd always wanted an icon of the Holy Innocents, and for her this became that. The connection between sainthood and inexplicable suffering is mysterious, but maybe that insight can help to dissolve some of my reactions to Arthur's periods of distress – the frantic desire to put right, the powerlessness before what seems hopelessly beyond help. Is staying with it more important than putting it right (see Chapter 5)? Even Jesus wept before Lazarus' tomb, and was overcome with violent emotion.

Yet still to come was another miraculous icon. The following April I went to Sweden to fulfil some lecturing engagements. One evening I found myself in an attic prayer room at the top of a historic country mansion, now a retreat house and Christian community centre. Present with others, I was unable to participate fully since the prayers were in Swedish. The room was full of icons, and as my eyes wandered from one to another I suddenly realized that I was looking at an icon of the raising of Lazarus. I became utterly riveted by it. Next morning, when not engaged, I quietly crept back up to that attic chapel and held the icon up to the light. It was dated 2009 and had been painted in Egypt in the traditional Coptic style, but facts like that are entirely secondary to its powerful impact on me. It brought final resolution to all the struggles of the past two years or so. I was deeply moved when it was presented to me as a parting gift and in lieu of fee – they'd realized how much more it would mean to me.

I was personally drawn into the icon by the body language of the women, their desperate pleas to Jesus, their tears and broken hearts – they were in the very place I'd been. Then behind them was the small figure of Lazarus, upright in the cave-like tomb above the coffin-box and tightly wrapped in swaddling-bands – the grave-clothes, so that he looked like a baby – indeed, like Jesus in nativity icons, yet he had an adult face, with a moustache, and an expression of not quite understanding: how could I not see my adult-baby, Arthur? And there, standing with arms raised, dominating the whole scene, was Jesus, calling Lazarus forth. But the women, distraught on the ground, clutching at Jesus' feet, or looking up to his face and pleading with tears, had no idea what Jesus was doing behind them. How could I know what Jesus was doing with Arthur behind my back? I was mercifully released from that need to be in control. I was finally able to let go, and maybe my letting go is Arthur's release – for in the story Jesus not only told Lazarus to come forth, but ordered others to 'loose him; let him go'. Arthur's been given his own life, and if I can move on, I too have been given my life back.

But as I explored the icon in the next few months, there'd be more. For now I'd finally found Jesus – the one I'd been looking for in the long watches of the night. Here was one larger than life, yet touching the most basic earthly realities of human living and dying. Here was a towering figure to whom I could entrust Arthur. Seven or eight months before, I'd been telling Jean Vanier about how well things were going for Arthur in his new place, and Jean had simply said, 'It just shows how much Jesus loves you, and Arthur, and Bob.' I'd been brought up short by the directness of it, and couldn't quite believe it, but now I knew it. And now too I'd discovered the face of Jesus. It was Andrew Teal who noticed in the icon the profound similarity between the face of Jesus and the face of Lazarus. But for me, Lazarus' face was Arthur. So face to face with Arthur, I could come face to face with Jesus, who in Christian tradition is the visible image of the invisible God. That insight I'm still exploring. Just at this point I received a copy of the book, *Saving Face*, by a former colleague, Stephen

Pattison. In a wide-ranging discussion, he draws out the mystery of persons and the significance of faces, then goes on to illuminate the parallel mystery of God, hidden and yet revealed, the one whose face no one can see and live; yet Moses spoke with God face to face as one speaks to a friend (see Chapter 2). In the past people did apparently see God; but in our culture, Stephen suggests, it's in one another's faces that God can be discerned, if we have eyes to see.

Jesus

He walked into my home;
  his eyes pierced
  my Martha soul.

He sat and conversed by the fire;
  his words scorched
  my Mary heart.

He bent over the bed;
  his touch raised
  my Lazarus smile.

The broken one he loved
  beyond us all.

So I think I've finally let go, and regained perspective – after all, for years I'd trusted others to care for Arthur while fulfilling professional engagements. New levels of detachment have paradoxically deepened love, for loving means not possessing but letting be (see Chapter 4). Sometimes when I visit, I can just gaze at Arthur's face. True eye contact is rare, but often a little smile hovers about his mouth and his eyes have a gentle shine, and I find myself falling in love again, just for who he is. And occasionally his smile, his chuckle, the light in his eyes when I arrive, lets me know that he does need me after all. In fact I'm at last beginning to believe the staff when they say he misses me; perhaps, for all our doubts, he is capable of more than recognition and does recall things. Certainly he's always had emotional moments when tears run down his cheeks – emotion of a very different quality from those periods of dry, tense distress. One wonders what it's about, acknowledging the deep mystery of his person. Tears and smiles – they touch my heart; they signify that our mutual need persists. Thanks be to God.

7

Arthur's vocation

------◆◆◆------

Silent Word

A man with a message?

Half-focused eyes look up to the sky
Through long thin fingers, gently splayed
And slowly waved, like flesh-tinged twigs
Obliquely catching light from the sun –
Not grasping, demanding or easily bored,
Just intrigued by fingers, moving arcs,
Shifting pointers, naked trees,
The trac'ry of pylons, slats of blinds,
Shafts of sunlight through winter clouds –
Not having, not doing, but being more.
Flickering smiles flit over his face,
Cheerful hands find each other in claps,
Then fingers fold in a gentle clasp,
Soon to re-open, long and thin –
Signposts through shadows to scattered light:

Yes – a gentle man with a message.

Arthur's young carer said more than once, 'He's a real gentleman.'
Not long afterwards came a phone call from a friend. She'd not seen
Arthur in person for years, but had a recent photograph in her hand.
'He's a man with a message,' she said; 'his photo is an icon in itself.'
Both comments struck me. Partly it was to do with his manhood.
Despite his moustache and increasingly bald head I was still trapped
in a mother–child relationship, dominated by responding to basic
needs – caring, washing, feeding; deciding for him, defending his
interests, taking the initiative, shaping his world; occasionally pleased

that he had a life of his own beyond home at the Day Centre, that he knew people I didn't know; but at some level unable to accept his maturity, his being a man. But it was also to do with who he is as a man – 'a gentleman', 'a man with a message'. True, I had over the years pondered his vocation, not least how it was part of my own ministry as I articulated insights given through him and others like him. But 'a gentle man with a message': what would that message be?

The photograph which triggered the comment was one of a series taken by Peter and Mary Humble, who were with us for Arthur's last weekend at home. Many of those images capture his hands, and so many people have noticed those fingers. His uncle calls them 'pianist's hands'. Pondering those comments and treasuring them in my heart, I naturally pictured those fingers, and slowly the poem emerged, a celebration of what it means to be alive and aware.

For Arthur offers not just a single message, but a handful of finger-posts pointing to various aspects of human existence and its meaning. We can see this as we gather up signals anticipated in earlier chapters. Fundamentally what he directs us to is not about competence – those hands with their intriguing patterns of movements have never even picked up a spoon and used it efficiently. Nor is it about acquiring things – it's always been so difficult to buy presents for Arthur since he makes use of nothing but that old favourite rattle in the shape of a hammer. Basically it's about appreciation, fascination, vaguely seeing yet not seeing, cheerfully being, just existing with a never-ending capacity for wonder at the same simple things.

That in itself may be the most significant message: a contemplative simplicity made infinitely problematic for most of us by our over-active consciousness and need for novel stimulation. But I guess if we follow Arthur's various pointers we'll find yet more rich reflections.

Fingerpost 1: pointing towards truly human values

The values of our culture are focused on success and achievement. Celebrity is celebrated, and the principal measure of worth is market-price. Statements about mission and values are produced by every kind of organization and, while the predominant tone may be about customer service, value for money is a significant driver. In most fields of employment, even in health, education and the churches, appraisal systems measure competence, while enhanced productivity is continually sought for the sake of cost-effectiveness. It's no accident that care-workers are badly paid and undervalued, while bankers take bonuses for granted. The economic worth of everything even affects relationships. So easily can they become short term, exploit-ative, manipulative, careless or patronizing, among colleagues, with clients, between patient and carer, even sometimes within marriage. Value in terms of success, particularly economic success, shapes the common sense of a culture motivated by the glory of achievement, whether in sport or showbiz, business or academe. Achievement brings reward – but non-achievers, even moderate achievers, are undermined. In my experience failure is what we fear, and a failure is how too many students feel because they haven't achieved as expected. All of us are infected by these values.

In such a culture, what value does Arthur have? None, by common-sense measures. And yet, might not he and others like him have a vocation to enable that shift in values which we outlined earlier (see Chapter 4), away from individualism, dominance, competitiveness, to community, mutuality – a human ecology which has the potential to be 'angelic'? What really makes us human is the capacity to ask for help, and that challenges modern claims to autonomy, as well as our individualism and success-values. The spirituality of the L'Arche communities has much to teach us about the presence of God in the everyday experience of living with persons who have learning disabilities. It's important to highlight the mutuality of this relation-ship. It's not a matter of doing good, or patronizing charity, but of receiving as well as giving, according dignity to the other person by receiving from them. The fruits of the Spirit, according to St Paul, are love, joy, peace, patience, kindness, generosity, faithfulness, gentle-ness and self-control (Gal. 5.22). It is in community with persons who are limited in their competence and capacity, at least compared with most of us, that we often best discover these deeper values.

In a world where competence and success is highly valued, where the success of science has fostered the perception that all ills can be overcome, death endlessly postponed and suffering alleviated, where perfect bodies are nurtured and exposed, where there's been a reaction against bodily inhibitions and sexual repression, L'Arche has perceived beauty in incurably damaged bodies, treasure in vulner-able and fragile persons. In the everydayness of attending to bodily functions, the sanctity of bodies is recognized in a context in which their transformation is not through make-up or cosmetic surgery, diet or exercise, medicine or miracles, but through recognition of God's love and power in mutual need. It is no accident that washing one another's feet has been developed as a paraliturgy in the L'Arche communities, for here in community bodily dependence on one another is sanctified. The 'gift of the unlikely givers' is 'the capacity to ask for help'. It's not simply that the strong help the weak; rather, those like Arthur reveal our common essential vulnerability as human creatures, and demonstrate that those fruits of the Spirit are both divine gift and at the same time truly human values.

So Arthur is the *gēr*, the outsider who enables us to enter into a redemptive relationship with one who is 'other', and reveals to us our own soul (see Chapter 5).

We too are helpless, in need of support. His uninhibited articulation of how he feels gives us permission, not only to weep with those who weep and rejoice with those who rejoice, but to acknowledge our own vulnerabilities, to allow ourselves to dissolve in tears. He challenges us, especially in his times of distress, to recognize that we are not always capable or in control, that all we can do when faced with human anguish is to stay with it, and trustingly depend on others and on God.

Fingerpost 2: pointing the way to the desert

Dependence, however, is the last thing that competent people want to admit, and to ensure that that prophetic message is taken to heart, Arthur leads us into the desert. Spiritual writers often speak of the need for displacement, for being shifted out of one's comfort zone, both to discover the depths within oneself and to meet God.

I had long since found the wilderness motif helpful when speaking of those years of doubt (see Chapter 2), but it was through Youakim Moubarac, a Lebanese Roman Catholic priest who participated in the first meeting of theologians at L'Arche, Trosly-Breuil, that my sense of the desert's significance was deepened. He offered a little paper in French which I had the privilege of translating for inclusion in the collection published under the title *Encounter with Mystery*. He wrote as a researcher come late to the spirituality of Syrian Antioch, telling how he focused on absolute solitude as a unique way of developing attachment to God. He asked himself,

'Is this ideal only accessible to a few?' And, assuming this to be the case, he wondered how even those fitted to it would fare in a world more and more urbanized, and where the desert places themselves are open to humankind's systematic exploitation of the planet. In pursuit of this he set himself to examine certain extreme states in modern existence: hospitalization, imprisonment, confinement in concentration camps. To these, he observed, Jean Vanier had added the handicapped condition, and had the audacity to think it a privileged place for meeting God. Moubarac noted that Aleksandr Solzhenitsyn, in *Cancer Ward*, had already revealed this possibility of meeting God *in extremis*, as had Boris Pasternak in *Dr Zhivago*. But he thought that the literature of L'Arche went even further, that it had effected a decisive turn in the course of Christian spirituality and had radically resolved the tension between contemplation and action for apostolic life. He explained:

> In as far as I understand Jean Vanier, daily dealings with people who have handicaps makes those involved face their own violence. Confronted by the irreducibility of the other, the one whom they mean to serve but whose condition they cannot ameliorate, they discover with horror that they are capable of striking them, or even wanting to do away with them. It is this, then, that I call a privileged desert place. The ancient anchorites took themselves off to the desert, they said, to fight with Satan on his own territory. We know now that it is enough to pay attention to the most defenceless people among us to find ourselves given up to our interior demons. But if only we force ourselves not to lose heart, if only grace comes to the aid of our weakness, we apprehend that to spend time with the poorest of all is not to do them charity, but to allow ourselves to be transformed by them and to apprehend God as gentleness.

This immediately rang bells with me, not just because of my own acquaintance with the literature of the desert as a scholar, but because of my own reactions when particularly challenged by Arthur's periods of distress. I recalled those long, bitter nights when he'd not slept, so neither had I, and that occasion when in sheer frustration I had given vent to my feelings by hurling a pillow on to the foot of his bed with force (well away from doing any actual harm). The inner demons were exposed: self-pity, anxiety about not sleeping with a heavy day of commitments ahead, the helplessness that comes from lack of control over the situation and not knowing what to do – yes, there was concern for him and his discomfort, desire to put things right for him if only I knew how, but it was overlaid by so many self-oriented passions. I discovered to my shame that I understood how some parents could batter their babies.

That was a graphic instance of the truth being exposed, but not the only time that Arthur has been the catalyst for discovering the profoundly ambiguous nature of that anxiety which passes for love. In tales of the early monks, the desert exposed their lack of single-minded reliance on God, as the wilderness had long before when the Israelites complained during their 40 years of exodus wanderings. In John's Gospel, the presence of Jesus is a catalyst exposing the truth, and this process is one of judgement, separating light from darkness; yet it was not for judgement, but salvation that Jesus came into the world (see Chapter 5). For without exposure, those inner demons cannot be cast out. The pain of self-discovery is an essential element in the process of being broken, moulded and renewed in God's image. It is something far more profound than our inner attempts to catalogue misdemeanours in routine prayers of confession, and it takes a catalyst or crisis for it to happen.

For Arthur to provoke this exposure means, of course, that he is at risk – even from those who love him. Abuse of persons with learning disabilities is all too common. A breaking scandal as we waited anxiously for Arthur's future to be resolved did little to assist my psychological adjustment to letting him go, to shift my profound lack of trust, in other people, in God (see Chapter 6). Yet the converse is Arthur's capacity to evoke fondness, to disperse depression, to tell us we're appreciated, we're beautiful, through the smile on his face and the light in his eyes – his own beauty. Long had I known how others grew fond of Arthur, long had I confessed that he ministered to me, diffusing the stresses of the day, enabling me to let everything go to focus on his basic human needs and his simple delight. It's no good being sentimental – those desperate nights were real as well. But when one of his new carers spoke of feeling down, then finding an answer to prayer as Arthur lifted his head from the pillow and smiled, I knew exactly what she meant. The desert is the place where you meet God. Meeting God involves judgement, but also joy and affirmation. By his 'otherness' and dependence Arthur engages those who relate to him, and leads them into this privileged desert place. He ministers to others on their pilgrim way.

Fingerpost 3: indicating the presence of Christ

When Arthur was a late teenager, I was invited to be the study leader for a week at the Othona Community in Bradwell-on-Sea in Essex. This community was founded immediately after the Second World War with the aim of peace and reconciliation, and every year groups of German students would come to share with a broad ecumenical group of all kinds of seekers and believers for the weeks of the summer. Arthur came with me for my stay. Every morning and evening people helped to get his wheelchair around the rough edge of a ploughed field to the chapel of St Peter's-on-the-Wall – the oldest place of Christian worship in England, built out of the stones and bricks of the old Roman fort of Othona, after which the community was named.

In the chapel, members took turns to lead prayer. Some people made up a scratch music group to lead the singing. One evening, in the candlelight, the person leading prayers said that he'd planned that we'd simply spend the time in silence. 'But with Arthur we cannot have silence,' he said. Arthur regularly responded to the echo of that old stone building by getting very excited and noisier and noisier, and he couldn't understand if you told him to be quiet; but with music he always quietly listened. So the worship leader said, 'We will create silence by singing Psalms.' The community has its own Psalm-book,[15] songs created from the biblical Psalms and other religious texts. Guitars and flutes and human voices echoed through the space as we sang one of them (the Othona version of Psalm 131), which went like this:

> I am too little, Lord,
>> to look down on others.
>
> I've not chased great affairs,
>> nor matters beyond me.
>
> I've tamed my wild desires
>> and settled my soul.
>
> My soul's a new fed child
>> at rest on the breast.
>
> My brothers seek the Lord,
>> both now and for ever.[16]

As we sang it suddenly seemed as if Arthur was the Christ-figure in our midst.

Over the years it's become ever clearer to me that there are aspects of the Body of Christ which can only be properly represented if persons with profound disabilities are incorporated into the Church's life, and Arthur's ministry to all of us is to make that point clear. Sometime back in the 1980s there was to be a day focusing on disability at the Queen's Theological College. I was asked to preach at the chapel service at the end. Being involved in worship at Queen's was part of my professional life on a weekday, and Arthur had never accompanied me then, as he regularly did and still does on Sundays. When I suggested I should arrange to bring him this was greeted with some consternation, expressed in the question, 'Why? Was he to be used as a visual aid?' I remember being quite taken aback, but also taking the question seriously in terms of examining my motives – there probably was an element of feeling people should confront the reality of what they had been talking about all day! But the more I thought about it the more I felt that Arthur's presence was essential to what I wanted to say on that occasion, and a compromise was reached: he would be taken out for the sermon, since there remained sensitivity about my talking about him in his presence – although the only thing he would have picked up was recognition of his own name, which he would probably then have repeated over and over again!

The whole incident sharpened up what I needed to say. 'There is neither Jew nor Greek, there is neither slave nor free, there is neither male nor female' (Gal. 3.28), and these days, I suggested, we would most of us naturally go on, 'black nor white, rich nor poor, Catholic nor Anglican, Orthodox nor Methodist, for you are all one in Christ Jesus.' But back then it was not so obvious that we would add reference to those with disabilities, and I challenged them with what had happened. I had received an invitation which gave me a sense not only of privilege but also of joy, because it provided an occasion when Arthur could join the worship of the community without a feeling of intrusion. This had been shattered, but this very shattering revealed the true meaning of his presence: it was a celebration of our wholeness together, and that celebration was essential to what I had to say. The trouble is that wholeness is associated with perfection – we imagine a state in which all loss and brokenness, all sin and pain and failure is wafted away, and it is that which we think is perfection. Disability seems to undermine that wholeness. But our wholeness in Christ is a wholeness that can absorb and transfigure loss, brokenness, disability, failure, sin, hurt and death – we become whole when we can live with the cross at the centre of the community.

Translations of the Bible are usually to be read aloud in public, and therefore for reasons of respectability sometimes fail to reveal exactly what the words convey. There is a case in point in the famous passage about the body of Christ in 1 Corinthians 12: 'the members of the body that seem to be weaker are indispensable,' reads the NRSV, 'and those members of the body we think less honourable we clothe with greater honour, and our less respectable members are treated with greater respect' (12.22–23). The Greek shows that this passage is actually talking about the body bits we are ashamed of or embarrassed about, those we cover up. Persons with severe learning disabilities still provoke reactions of embarrassment, and they are the least powerful people in our society, usually dependent and lacking autonomy, with little control over their circumstances. But it is precisely such persons who need to be included if the body of Christ is to be whole. We must honour what we might be ashamed of. Paul is anxious to affirm that he is not ashamed of the cross – in his society it meant the shame of condemnation, and it would not be long before Christians were lampooned by graffiti of a crucified ass. We must affirm the weak: the body of Christ is a physical image, and the physical reality was that in his bodily existence Christ was abused, disabled, and put to death. The resurrected Christ appeared with the marks of the nails.[17] Some aspects of God's image in Christ can only be reflected in the Church as the body of Christ by the full inclusion and honouring of those who have bodies that are likewise impaired.

This suggestion that the image of God can only be reflected in the body of Christ by the inclusion of damaged persons flies in the face of traditional presuppositions. In the history of Christian theology, the notion that humanity is made in the image of God has been interpreted in elitist and individualistic terms. My argument would be that the image of God is to be found fully only in Christ, and that its thrust is corporate.

Traditionally it's been assumed that the image of God is to be found in the human intellect. The mind or soul is in God's image, since the bodily (corporeal or physical) aspect of human nature can hardly represent the incorporeal, spiritual reality of the transcendent God. We shouldn't underestimate the profound reaction against idolatry in early Christianity: no animal or human form should be taken to represent God who is invisible. By contrast, the perceived kinship between the human mind and God's Mind (or *Logos*), coupled with the analogy between the Incarnation of God's Word (or *Logos*) in Christ and the embodiment of the soul/mind in the human person, encouraged a predominantly intellectual interpretation of how human beings are made in the image of God. This tendency may at times have permitted the positive acceptance of intelligent persons with physical disabilities: for example, Didymus the Blind (fourth century) was nicknamed Didymus the See-er because he saw more profoundly than those with physical sight. It has sometimes encouraged positive (if somewhat patronizing) responses to persons with profound mental disabilities on the grounds that 'you can see the soul peeping out through their eyes'. But is that really true? This approach is not only elitist but also dualist in its soul-body understanding of human nature, and ultimately tends to exclude those, like Arthur, whose mental or physical incapacities significantly challenge that viewpoint, since their physical being profoundly affects their entire personality and existence (see Chapter 2).

In the more recent history of Christian theology, the notion that humanity is made in the image of God has tended to have an individualistic interpretation. It's taken to mean that each of us is made in the image of God, and therefore each of us deserves to be equally respected. It conspires with modern 'human rights' ideologies to encourage individuals to assert their right to a decent deal in society, and to recognition of each person's inherent dignity, no matter what their race, religion or impairment. This tendency has had positive impact in encouraging respect for those who are not white, male, able-bodied and intelligent. But it has also exacerbated the prejudice that we should all be perfect since we are made in God's image. Obvious failure to reach such notional perfection then becomes problematic. How can this person, who apparently has physical or mental defects, be made in God's image? The modernist rights approach may challenge the attitudes of some past traditional societies, but the success-oriented values of modern individualism encourage an interpretation of what it means to be in God's image which, I would argue, does not take account of core elements in Christian theology.

So let's reconsider what it means to be made in the image of God by returning to Scripture. The phrase occurs in the Genesis narrative of the creation of Adam. So there are two important features to note. First, Adam represents the whole human race – the very name Adam means Man, that is, in the sense of 'humanity', for the creation of Eve from his rib represents the subsequent sexual differentiation in the human race. Second, Adam is indeed described as made in the image and likeness of God, but the story that follows tells how this was marred by his disobedience, classically known as the Fall. So glib theological talk about being made in God's image needs to be countered with a sensitivity to the corporate nature of that image, and the fact that all have fallen short of the glory (image) of God (Rom. 3.23).

This reflection on Genesis 1 is confirmed by the New Testament. A reading of Paul's epistles soon shows that the dynamic of salvation depends upon the parallel between Adam and Christ. Adam is the 'old man', Christ the 'new man' (Rom. 5; 2 Cor. 5.17), and all of us (male and female) are in Adam and potentially in Christ (Rom. 7; 1 Cor. 15.22). Both are in some sense corporate figures. In Christ we are a new creation, but as in Adam all die, so in Christ all will be made alive. In a sense Christ alone is the true image of God – the image of God in Adam (the old humanity) was marred. So we are only in God's image if we are in Christ, and it is by baptism that we are incorporated into him. It has always been of the greatest importance to me that Arthur was baptized as a baby – even though he cannot receive the sacrament or make a profession of the faith, he is held in God's grace and belongs to the body of Christ.

The body of Christ is essentially a corporate image – a body is made up of many members, all of whom bring different contributions to the whole (1 Cor. 12; Rom. 12). Indeed, as already noted, the weak limbs (members), and even those body bits we are ashamed of and cover up, are indispensable and are to be especially honoured; and because in his bodily existence Christ was abused, disabled and put to death, some aspects of God's image in Christ can only be reflected in the Church as the body of Christ by the full inclusion and honouring of those who have bodies that are likewise impaired.

The founder of L'Arche, Jean Vanier, often speaks of brokenness (see Chapter 3). I once became fascinated by the fraction of the communion wafer – coming from a tradition which simply uses bread for Communion I was struck by the sharp sound of the cracking. Perhaps the breaking of the body of Christ is necessary for the Church to be the Church. Only after the fraction can the broken pieces be gathered again into the one loaf. As the Spirit of the living God breaks and moulds each of us, so the Church has to suffer the pain of brokenness so as to be humbled and ready to welcome those impaired. Christ had no form or comeliness – the broken crucified body was scarcely a pretty sight, hardly something to be welcomed. Those like Arthur who have profound disabilities sometimes enable that shock to be felt. Maybe that is their prophetic vocation.

Fingerpost 4: pointing to the Beyond

It is difficult to know what Arthur takes in, given his lack of language. It makes one aware of how much language shapes our experience: after all, we identify what we see or hear by naming each thing and so distinguishing it from other things in our vision or hearing. The process of naming differentiates; the significant is highlighted and other things recede into the background, often not noticed.

I once found myself contemplating the question of how exactly Arthur experiences the world without the possibility of such articulation. He certainly recognizes faces and places, and knows his regular routines. Sounds and music delight him, especially the human voice, as do patterns of light. The first word he attempted to copy was 'trees', and like trees pylons and suspended wires attract his attention as dark patterns against a light sky. He remains 'echolalic' (as his final school report put it), and perhaps associates 'car' with going out for a ride, and 'down' with being moved from his wheelchair to the beanbag. But since he sometimes just delights in articulating one or other of his limited range of 'words' at quite inappropriate moments, it is hard to know what he does understand (see Chapter 1).

So what possible sense does he make of the average church service? Most obviously he responds to music, as already illustrated. The light of recognition comes into his face if I sing 'Away in a manger' or one of the nursery rhymes that he heard repeatedly as a baby. At home I've watched his reactions change with the tempo and mood of the music on the radio; *Songs of Praise* is his favourite TV programme; and in church you can see him listening. Human voices singing hymns stimulate response in him. He also reacts to big open spaces, and especially anything patterned in light: I shall never forget the wonder on his face when we took him into Salisbury Cathedral and he gazed up at the vaulted ceiling as the organ began to play. He seems to respond to atmosphere – though it is when the music stops that he thinks it's his turn to join in, and if the music has made him excited his often noisy articulation precludes silence. Some congregations are capable of accepting that he is praising God in his own way, though one must admit that others find his presence distracting and disturbing, especially if not used to his behaviour.

My reflections on how he perceives the world were summed up in this poem:

> Imagine a life with sound but no word –
> A life full of music and buzzing and shouts
> But no structure or form. Could meaning be there
> At all, or would everything be absurd?
>
> Imagine a life with sight but no sense –
> A life full of colour and movement and shapes
> But no objects or space. Wouldn't it seem
> A random muddle, a jumble immense?
>
> But patterns are there, and proportion discerned
> In the slatted light of Venetian blinds,
> In the fractals of trees or the web of a grille:
> So some sense of beauty is learned.
> Yet much blindness remains, and still there's a kind
> Of incomprehension that shuts off the mind.
>
> And expressions are there, and moods conveyed
> In the tone of voices, in laughter, in tears:
> In music's dynamics, its beat and its flow –
> So some connection is made.
> Yet much deafness remains, and still there's a kind
> Of incomprehension that shuts off the mind.
>
> Perception has limits. Our brain-damaged son
> Lives a life full of colour and music and light,
> A life full of loving and sharing and fun,

153

But really perception has hardly begun.
He has such limitations – yet still there's a kind
Of mysterious awareness enlarging the mind.

Perception has limits – our vision's too small.
As for loving and sharing, our failures appal.
We have such limitations – but still there's a kind
Of mysterious transcendence enlarging the mind.

This poem may shift us on to consider the whole question of language in worship, for it suggests that what we have to do with in worship is quite beyond us, and that Arthur's limitations enable us to recognize our own.

Worship goes beyond words. Twentieth-century liturgical revisions, along with multiple updated translations of the Bible, seem to imply that we are supposed to understand. But if we think we can comprehend God, then God is reduced to the size of our own minds. This is a point made repeatedly by the early Fathers and theologians of the Church; indeed, Ephrem the Syrian, in his remarkable theological poetry, suggested that the Incarnation of God's Word was not just in flesh, but in human language. God had to accommodate the divine self to our level, and speak to us in our terms. So he clothed the divine self in all kinds of metaphors and symbols. It was like someone trying to teach a parrot to speak while hiding behind a mirror so that the parrot thought it was speaking with one of its own kind.[18]

The inadequacy of human language for the truth about God is fundamental to theology, and the attempt to put the whole truth into words conspires with attitudes to Scripture which reduce it to narrowly literal reference. There is a parable that does the rounds which invites us to imagine what sense a two-dimensional creature would make of our three-dimensional world, so as to stimulate us into appropriate humility; maybe there is a fourth dimension out there which is just as real but with our creaturely limitations we cannot perceive it. That same humility may be fostered by relationship in worship with someone like Arthur, by consciousness of the limitations in his perception of which we are aware and he is not, by deep identification with that reality of not being able to put the sacred into words or grasp it. Liturgy is in any case more than words – the words both point beyond themselves and are performative, so that the liturgy is an *act* of worship. Arthur reminds us that we are caught up in something bigger than ourselves – certainly bigger than our words, and bigger than our understanding.

I suggest that this may also have something to say about the propensity of those who lead worship to 'talk down' to children or outsiders, or to people who have little theological sophistication. People who sense a patronizing approach will be turned off just as much as if things appear strange, foreign and incomprehensible. We might learn from the fact that no adaptation can get things down to Arthur's level. Far more important is the generation of the kind of atmosphere which makes people feel they are caught up in something totally beyond every one of us – a transcendent and healing mystery, which summons us out of our self-preoccupation and enables us to become incorporated into something bigger than ourselves.

Not all persons with learning disabilities are as incapacitated with language as Arthur is, but many operate with a very simple level of linguistic competence. I am impressed by the fact that in the worship at the L'Arche community in Trosly-Breuil there is no compromise over the liturgy of the Mass. In their plain stone chapel, created out of an old barn, there are songs with guitars and simple sung responses, but also the long lections, a homily and intercessions that are usual everywhere. It is, of course, in the vernacular French – Latin having been superseded since Vatican II – but it is just as wordy as any other Mass or Eucharist. Few of those present are likely to follow all that much. Yet the sheer sense of habitude and familiarity, of togetherness and presence, creates an atmosphere to which the inarticulate sounds of those with profound disabilities seem to contribute; and some with a slightly higher level of competence, despite their considerable impairments, receive the immense sense of dignity and worth that comes from the privilege of serving at the altar. I remember, too, the worship in the chapel at the old Monyhull Hospital, an institution for those with learning disabilities now closed because of changes in policy. In a service deliberately following liturgies used elsewhere in the Church, so that here too there was sharing in the one body of Christ, people with little or no language would rush to the altar rail to receive the sacrament with a simple 'thank you', somehow sensing the depth of what was happening.

The sense of sacred place, atmosphere and music may be more important than words for creating worship. That is not to say that words do not matter – for most of us they do, and for all of us the human voice is key to the sense of shared experience. But worship needs to transcend words, and praise may be expressed in 'songs without words'. Arthur helps us to recognize that our language is groping and inadequate when it comes to the Beyond.

Fingerpost 5: pointing to the mystery of grace

I have spoken of being taken up into something bigger than ourselves. I would like to suggest that that is not a bad definition of worship. 'You have made us for yourself,' said St Augustine, 'and our heart is restless till it rests in you.'[19] It implies that participation in worship is more to do with receptivity than with contributing.

In recent decades there's been much drive to get more people to participate in worship by playing an active part, reading lessons, or offering intercessions. Does this really mean greater participation? Individuals who do these things may feel a greater sense of dignity and worth, and the congregation may feel they represent them in an important sense; but on the other hand, these individuals may be nervous, and their performance may therefore not assist anybody, including themselves, to be caught up in something bigger. Participation in a concert or in the theatre does not mean going on stage yourself. It means responding to what is going on so as to be involved in the action or the music, taken beyond in a way that leads to self-forgetfulness. Great preaching is like great acting, in the sense that it claims attention and moves people to respond, to see things differently, to change their attitudes, to live in a different imaginative world which provides a larger perspective within which to discover meaning and live out their day-to-day lives. Great music can lift the spirit to inner realms of wordless worship, even more effectively than singing ourselves – though hymn-singing is for many the main experience of actual participation in corporate worship.

I want to suggest that the presence of Arthur in worship reinforces this point. How does Arthur participate? Mainly by his silence and the rapture on his face when singing is lifting his spirit. Sometimes by echoing the intonation of the preacher's voice, or shouting his own name. Often by vigorous hand-clapping. Yes, he is less inhibited than most of us – but the point surely remains, even if our responses are internal and private rather than overt. Participation happens at all kinds of levels and in all kinds of ways. The sermon may not impact on Arthur in the same way as it does the elderly retired headmaster whose intellect is engaged, and who needs some stimulating thoughts to feed his mind as well as his heart. The whole point about liturgy is that it stimulates participation and feeds people differently. The aim of worship is to generate the kind of participation which takes people out of themselves so that they become more truly themselves in the larger whole.

Arthur's contribution is small and potentially disruptive. That may in itself be a gift to the rest of us, jerking us out of habit into a new depth. But the question now is what does he receive – what is God doing in him in worship? It is impossible to know – a mystery of grace, which nevertheless has its signs in the responses I have described. He would not receive the communion elements even if offered them – feeding him has never been straightforward! Sometimes he even resists a blessing – too many have forced their touch upon him in public settings. Yet somehow grace is mediated, and so being with him may help us to recognize that what we do matters less than being bathed, like him, in the music of voices and the smiles of presences, in a sense of abandonment to the sensations of sounds and sight, even bodily movement, as we receive grace through the mediation of the liturgical actions and through one another. What happens to any of us remains elusive; too often we invest too much in what we are conscious of – in 'feelings' of response. Arthur reminds us that often we may well receive grace without being fully aware of the fact, and there is much more to receive than we can know. Through him we discern that in the vocation of love, as one friend put it, being loved comes first.

Conclusion

Someone once commented to me that 'Arthur's presence in church is gospel', and indeed I've learned over the years that Arthur, though not of course officially ordained by the Church, is nevertheless a minister. I've come to believe that persons with even the most profound limitations have a vocation to be a 'sign' in the biblical sense: a prophetic sign, pointing beyond themselves. Turning from one fingerpost to another, and seeing their connections, we can articulate how Arthur is such a sign:

- He reveals to us, so-called 'normal' people, something about who we truly are: we are vulnerable creatures, and it is when our vulnerability shows up our dependence on one another that true community is discovered and the fruits of the Spirit can mature: love, joy, peace, patience, kindness, generosity, faithfulness, gentleness and self-control (Gal. 5.22).

- He summons us to deeper self-knowledge and true humility in the presence of the God who transcends all human language and conceptuality, offering a model of patient wonder at the most ordinary everyday familiar things – of contemplative appreciation.

- He bears witness to the Christ who had 'no form or comeliness' (Isa. 53.2), no beauty to attract us, but was despised and rejected, ensuring that that image is included as one facet of the body of Christ.

- He speaks to us of a wholeness which incorporates our impairments, of a transcendence that does not negate the cross any more than the resurrection wafts it away with a magic wand, of an hour of glory in which all our darkness and 'gone-wrongness' is embraced, entered and borne, and so transformed.

- He shows us that worship is more about the grace and love we receive than anything we do, that it is fundamentally about being caught up in something bigger than ourselves, and that it is most deeply to be found in 'songs without words'. At one time people imagined that the cosmic spheres created music, and so this heavenly harmony offered ceaseless praise of the Creator. The Psalms remind us that in worship we enter the wordless praise of the whole of creation:

> Praise him, sun and moon; praise him, all you shining stars!
> Praise him, you highest heavens . . .
> Mountains and all hills, fruit trees and all cedars!
> Wild animals and all cattle, creeping things and flying birds! . . .
> Let them praise the name of the LORD,
>   for his name alone is exalted;
>   his glory is above earth and heaven.   (Ps. 148.3, 4, 9, 10, 13)

Just to be is to respond to the One who made us, redeems us, loves us. Arthur calls us to that humbling awareness. Thanks be to God.

Afterword

There are moments of transition that dramatically focus something core to our life, or confront us, or hone us, or form us more into the persons we are meant to be.

If I reflect upon my experience of 'being called into fuller life', I find, slightly to my surprise, that Arthur and his family have been axiomatic in helping me to discern what a vocation to inhabit my life more truly might be. Sister Barbara June, a member of the Community of the Sisters of the Love of God, put it more succinctly: 'Arthur has been a funnel for your vocation.'

I first became aware of Arthur without even knowing his name. A sermon preached by his mother at the Queen's College, Birmingham, and broadcast one snowy Advent Sunday in (I think) 1979 on BBC Radio 4, spoke about recognizing the characteristic hallmarks of God's own presence in Jesus. It began with the provocative lines:

> If you should happen to see God walking down the street to meet you, how would you recognize him? Well, I know silly questions deserve silly answers, so what if you saw a familiar friend, how would you recognize that person?

It's by recognizable characteristics that we're able to identify people we know, the preacher suggested, and even though we 'cannot see God and live' (Exod. 33.20), God's self-disclosure through the biblical story enables us to identify the characteristics which signal God's encounter with us in our lives, if we have eyes to see and ears to hear. She then spoke movingly of knowing 'a woman in Christ who had seen God coming down the street to meet her'.

> She didn't recognize him at first, but on reflection the characteristic marks of God's presence were there. This woman has a profoundly disabled son, and something had happened to make her feel that her son was not acceptable. Dejected, she pushed him across a park when an old priest came hobbling along and met her. He passed the time of day, spoke to her son kindly, and continued on his way. [Here were]

159

words of acceptance, words of grace. The characteristic marks of God in Christ were there.

The words were, of course, autobiographical. They voiced the agony of a mother dejected at her son's exclusion, but also invited hearers into an understanding of God's freedom and presence to creation and to honour and reverence Arthur's worth. The articulate address plumbed human woundedness, exposing at one and the same time God's intimate and loving participation in creaturely life. The preacher's sermon allowed Arthur's life and experience to illustrate that there is nowhere in the human condition, neither pleasure nor despair, where God is not authentically, and truly, present.

It was to a very large degree this powerful and authoritative address that made me eschew other universities and go to Birmingham to read theology. Once there, as an earnest if naive undergraduate, with friends I responded to the invitation to look after Arthur and his brothers from time to time for weekends. The sermon ceased to be extrinsic words about someone, and took flesh. The experiences were as fun as they were demanding – punctuated by learning and enjoying Arthur's mischievous delight as he would sweep his arm across the table to send plates of food left within his grasp on to the floor before laughing with joy. Sharing human laughter is profoundly humanizing, as was being drawn into Arthur's transcendental delight as he shook his hammer rattle, or responded to various rebuking exclamations of 'Oh, Arthur!'

In all this mix, I became aware of a living, authentic Mystery in the network of relationships with Arthur: there was the dignity of encountering another person whose needs are profound as my equal, indeed nurturing my own need for humanity and direction without the din of words in a real relationship. No doubt this can sound overly sentimental – and that would be a betrayal of the discomfort and pain Arthur has known (and the worry, dilemmas and concerns of his family); but there were profound moments of silent awareness of an invitation into authenticity: Arthur's vulnerability and his integrity cohered.

In the garden one sunny afternoon, I sat reading a theology text, while Arthur just sat, attending to and inhabiting the moment with integrity and an authenticity that I became aware I lacked for many reasons. It was nowhere near a sense of being accused or diminished.

On the contrary, Arthur simply sat, in the speckled sunlight under the trees, the light and shadow dancing as a breeze moved the leaves above him, and he held up his hands and looked at the moving kaleidoscopic light and shade through his fingers. Such a simple engagement recapitulated so much of that attentive inhabiting of creatureliness that we style 'holiness' – much more articulate an exposition than pages of discourse. Hilary of Poitiers put it like this:

> Faith ought, in silence, to . . . worship the Father, reverence with him the Son, abounding in the Holy Spirit, but we must strain the poor resources of our language to express thoughts too great for words. The error of others compels us to err in daring to embody in human terms truths which ought to be hidden in the silent veneration of the heart.

The engagement with Arthur's life and 'the silent veneration of his heart' has been a powerful renewing and redirecting force in my life at many turns. He has, for all his obvious disabilities, invited me, no doubt among many others, into a life more true. He has been a conduit of God's vocation – and the characteristic hallmarks of God's presence are there: a still welcome, no desire to manipulate or possess, moments of truthful, joyful engagement; and his inhabiting of the moment beckons us – and will always be a prompt for me – to move authentically into a quality of life that prioritizes dignity and compassion.

Arthur remains an authentic compass – his presence and friendship shaped my exploration into Anglican ministry, as well as adventures into the academy – and he signifies a profound openness to the unexpected: an openness mediated by his cupped hands and open fingers dancing with the light and shadow of that summer's day.

Arthur's vocation and provocation is clear to me – he shows that we are as prone to Love as the sun is to shine.

Andrew Teal

Notes

1 Scripture Union, *Encounter with God*, Bible reading notes for 7 August 2013.
2 Young (1979).
3 Donald Allchin in Young (1997), p. 108.
4 Midgley (1995), p. 198.
5 Seabright (2010).
6 The quotations in this paragraph are drawn from Weil (1974).
7 Weil (1974), pp. 80ff.
8 Lennox (2007), p. 47, italics in original.
9 See Vanstone (1982).
10 Crossan (1988).
11 This paragraph melds together insights from Exum (1992) and Nussbaum (1986).
12 MacKinnon (1979), p. 194.
13 Tillich (1978), vol. 2, pp. 172f.
14 Pseudo-Macarius, *Homily* 47.15.
15 Hodgetts (1976).
16 From *The Othona Psalms*, copyright © Colin Hodgetts 1976. Used with permission.
17 Eiseland (1994) explores this point.
18 Brock (1992).
19 *Confessions* I.1.

References

This section lists the books to which I've made reference in the text or footnotes, arranged by chapter for easy reference.

1 Arthur's life with us

Young, Frances, 'Family Forum: What is the purpose of it all?', *Apex: Journal of the British Institute of Mental Handicap*, vol. 7 no. 2, 1979, p. 52. Reprinted in the *Yearbook of the Birmingham Society for Mentally Handicapped Children*, 1981.

2 Through the wilderness years

Hick, John, *Evil and the Love of God*, London: Macmillan, 1966.

3 L'Arche, Lourdes, and Faith and Light

Vanier, Jean, *Community and Growth*, London: Darton, Longman and Todd, 1979.

Young, Frances (ed.), *Encounter with Mystery: Reflections on L'Arche and Living with Disability*, London: Darton, Longman and Todd, 1997.

4 Creation

Crossan, John Dominic, *The Dark Interval: Towards a Theology of Story*, Sonoma, CA: Polebridge Press, 1988.

Lennox, John C., *God's Undertaker: Has Science Buried God?* Oxford: Lion, 2007.

MacIntyre, Alasdair, *Dependent Rational Animals: Why Human Beings Need the Virtues*, 2nd edn, London: Duckworth, 2009.

Midgley, Mary, *Beast and Man: The Roots of Human Nature*, rev. edn, London: Routledge, 1995.

Seabright, Paul, *The Company of Strangers: A Natural History of Economic Life*, rev. edn, Princeton, NJ: Princeton University Press, 2010.

Vanstone, W. H., *The Stature of Waiting*, London: Darton, Longman and Todd, 1982.

Weil, Simone, *Gateway to God: A Selection from the Writings of Simone Weil*, ed. David Raper, London: Fontana, 1974.

5 The cross and redemption

Douglas, Mary, *Purity and Danger*, London: Routledge and Kegan Paul, 1966.

Eliot, T. S., *Murder in the Cathedral*, London: Faber and Faber, 1935.

Exum, J. Cheryl, *Tragedy and Biblical Narrative*, Cambridge: Cambridge University Press, 1992.

MacKinnon, Donald, *Explorations in Theology* 5, London: SCM Press, 1979.

Nietzsche, F., *The Birth of Tragedy*, trans. W. A. Haussmann, London: Allen and Unwin, 1909.

Nussbaum, Martha, *The Fragility of Goodness*, Cambridge: Cambridge University Press, 1986.

Tillich, Paul, *Systematic Theology*, London: SCM Press, 1978.

Young, Frances M., *Sacrifice and the Death of Christ*, London: SPCK, 1975.

6 Loving and letting go

Pattison, Stephen, *Saving Face: Enfacement, Shame, Theology*, Farnham: Ashgate, 2013.

Pozzo di Borgo, Philippe, Jean Vanier and Laurent de Cherisey, *Tous Intouchables?* Montrouge Cedex: Bayard, 2012.

7 Arthur's vocation

Brock, Sebastian, *The Luminous Eye*, 2nd edn, Kalamazoo, MI: Cistercian Publications, 1992.

Eiseland, Nancy, *The Disabled God: Towards a Liberation Theology of Disability*, Nashville, TN: Abingdon Press, 1994.

Hodgetts, Colin, *The Othona Psalms*, Bradwell-on-Sea: The Othona Community, 1976.

8 Afterword

McKenna, Stephen, *St Hilary of Poitiers: The Trinity*. The Fathers of the Church Patristic Monograph Series, Washington, DC: Catholic University of America Press, 2002.